GIANT
EARTH-MOVING
EQUIPMENT

Eric C. Orlemann

Motorbooks International
Publishers & Wholesalers

To my wife, Beth,
for the patience and understanding you have given me during this entire project.

Library of Congress Cataloging-in-Publication Data
Orlemann, Eric C.
    Giant earth-moving equipment/Eric C. Orlemann.
        p. cm.
    Includes index.
    ISBN 0-7603-0032-1
    1. Earthmoving machinery. I. Title.
TA725.069   1995
629.225—dc20   95-14010

On the front cover: A Marion 5860 stripping shovel, working at CONSOL's Truax Traer's Burning Star No. 3 mine in 1966, unloads over 120 tons of overburden from its 80cu-yd dipper.

On the frontispiece: Though it looks like something from a science-fiction movie set, it's actually an O&K BWE 289 "Central Tower" type bucket wheel excavator. The largest earth-moving machines operating today are of this style. *Krupp Fördertechnik*

On the title page: O&K's RH200E is powered by a massive 1600kW/2146hp electric motor. *Orenstein & Koppel*

On the back cover: Color photo: Marion 5900 stripping shovel takes a big bite of planet earth. *Marion INDESCRO* Black & white photo: Mining companies once held open houses to show off their latest big diggers. This one occurred in Ohio in 1967. *Dale Davis collection*

Printed in China

Contents

Acknowledgments

IN THE PREPARATION OF THIS book project over the last thirty-two months, many individuals have given their time and access to resources that I am truly grateful for. Through the course of the research, I have probably tried the patience of many individuals in asking a seemingly endless amount of questions. It would be hard to tell, though, since I only received the utmost cooperation from the manufacturers, the mining companies, and other individuals within the industry.

The author would like to extend his sincerest thanks to: William A. Borthwick, George Kenyon, William Daly, James Rosso, Bob Muntz, Mary Whitledge, Pete J. Holman, Steve Newhouse, Jeff Hawkinson, Tom Novak, David Zimmermin, William E. Bontemps, Peter Gilewicz, Tom Lusch, Bill Williams, Larry Runnoe, George Patrick, Joel Grace, Rudy J. Sudrla, Steve Khail, Peter Winkel, Pete Benger, J. Peter Ahrenkiel, Paul Wild, H. Schwarz, Doug Walker, Dale Davis, Dorothy J. Hammer, Daniel M. Gaynor, D. Dallheimer-May, Martha Glasgow, Roger Hull, Robert Schaffer, Jon Kus, Frank D. Page, David Stein, John Cunningham, and the writings of Peter Grimshaw.

Thanks to the following mining operations and individuals for specially requested location photography and information: Christine L. Taylor, Peabody Holding Co. Inc.; Sue Tucker, P&M Coal Mining Co.; Ruth A. Olney and Hubert C. Place, Arch Mineral Corp./Arch of Illinois; David Douglas, D. Jenkins, Dave Scott, Green Coal Co.; Kevin Feeney, Julie L. Lewis, and Jeffrey L. Vandiver, Amax Coal Co.; Joe Cerenzia, Les Delloma, Mike Torchik, and Donald G. Gibson, CONSOL Inc.; Dave Waitkus and James C. Patton, AEP Fuel Supply/Central Ohio Coal Co.

I am also indebted to the following organizations and individuals for additional photography assistance and research information: Don Frantz and Keith Haddock, Historical Construction Equipment Association; Vicky Johnson, Big Brutus Inc.; Bruce Kurschenska, Images West; Don DeCoursey, Jr., Kehres Photo; and A.C. Color Lab Inc.

My biggest thanks goes to Alvin E. Nus, without whose early help and insight this book would not have been possible.

Eric C. Orlemann
Cleveland
1995

Specifications

THE SPECIFICATIONS REFERRED TO THROUGHOUT this book are all in standard US English SAE weights and measures. All reference to a machine's weight in tons is calculated at 2,000 pounds (lb) per short ton. Usage of any metric specifications is identified as such. The average weight of a cubic yard of material is rated at 3,000lb. But because of material density variances—such as a cubic yard of coal, which is rated at about 1,400– 1,500lb—machines with extra capacity buckets have a much higher volume in cubic yards compared to standard versions. However, overall tonnage ratings remain the same. Equipment working with heavier material, such as iron ore at 4,000-5,400lb a cubic yard, would get lower-volume buckets and dippers.

Most terminology in the text is self-explanatory, but a few abbreviations that might need further clarification are as follows:

Gross hp: Gross horsepower (hp) is the output of the engine or motor as installed in the machine, without the major accessories connected.

fhp: Flywheel horsepower, sometimes referred to as net horsepower, is the actual horsepower output, with all accessories connected, including the fan, air compressor, generator, and hydraulic pump.

Introduction

STANDING AT THE BASE OF a gigantic stripping shovel, I was in awe at the sheer size and scope of such a man-made marvel. This machine had presence. It commanded your respect. This was not some fire-breathing monstrosity from a monster truck freak show. No, this was the real thing, a true mechanical dinosaur, able to take massive bites out of the earth's crust as it roams where few of us are able, or would care to go.

Yet for the men and women who work with these titans, they are something more than just "earthmoving" machines. Carrying distinctive names—Elza, Dakota Star, Big Geordie, The Silver Spade, Lady of the Lake, Freddy Flintstone, Sequoia, Brutus, Big Hog, The Captain, The GEM of Egypt, Big Muskie, The Tiger, The Green Hornet, The Wasp, Ursa Major, and dozens more—they start to take on their own distinct personalities, as did aircraft named by fighter and bomber crews in World War II.

The earthmoving equipment operators depend on these machines and the machines give their operators everything they have, often in the most treacherous working conditions one can imagine. You can always count on them coming through, no matter what the circumstances. They were and are a sense of pride to the operators, the workers, and to the companies that build and operate them.

For most of us, these machines are but pictures in an encyclopedia or a "Guinness Book of World Records". Many have already played out their lives and are but a memory held by the miners and construction workers who kept them going, sometimes for decades. But in our everyday lives we reap the benefits that these giants have helped provide. They uncover and load the coal that provides energy for our homes and industries. They unearth minerals such as gold, silver, copper, uranium, lead, zinc, iron, salt, and countless others that make up the jewelry we wear, the cars we drive, and the stereos we listen to. From high fashion to high tech, no industry can do without the massive amounts of minerals made accessible by these fantastic machines.

But what is it that attracts us to these giants? Maybe it's our fascination with machines that are the pinnacle in their class for size, power, and speed. It's not the plain Pontiac LeMans that is coveted, but the powerful GTO version instead. These machines we're examining are the things that are larger than life, making us ask the questions of how they were built, where

do they work, and inevitably, how much do they cost?

The different types of earthmoving equipment are all part of a large system of machines arranged for the most productive and economical use in a mining or heavy construction application. Each has a particular function, with some overlap in abilities, enabling the owners to maximize their considerable investment to the fullest. Also, the type of material that is being mined dictates the type of equipment that will be used. For instance, in the bituminous coal surface mining industry in the United States, large draglines or stripping shovels first remove the upper layers of earth (called "overburden") covering the coal seams. Smaller loading shovels are then brought in to load the coal into haulers of a rear dump or bottom dump nature.

A Marion 204-M Superfront shovel shows off its unique variable-pitch front end and 30cu-yd dipper in 1979.

The business end of the O&K RH200, showing off its 29cu-yd capacity, 15ft 5in width bullclam, with a rating of almost 44 tons of material per bucket load.

By contrast, in Europe, where lignite—often called "brown coal"—is mined, large bucket wheel excavators are used. Since the lignite is a softer type of coal and is found in less-rocky regions of the world, mass removal of the material, often employing large overland conveyers, is the answer.

Another factor in the production of these giants is their perceived economical necessity in the marketplace. After World War II, the demand for all types of products, from cars to washing machines, skyrocketed. More cars meant better and larger freeway systems. And to meet these needs, industry needed more energy and raw materials. So in the 1950s and on through the 1960s, larger and larger earthmoving machinery was required to dig the coal, build the dams, and lay the roads.

The earthmoving equipment industry had its ups and downs, but nothing could prepare these companies for what

Left
The Bucyrus-Erie 1950-B "Silver Spade" at work on a clear spring day in May 1994, at CONSOL's Mahoning Valley Mine No. 36 in Cadiz, Ohio.

happened to them in the 1970s and 1980s.

The oil embargo of 1973-1974 set off a chain of events that had everyone seeking ways to make the United States more self-sufficient in satisfying its energy needs. Oil exploration and the mining for larger coal sites were the most obvious solutions. Companies such as Marion Power Shovel and Bucyrus-Erie had large back orders for their shovels and draglines. The introduction of new equipment from Caterpillar, Terex, WABCO, Unit Rig, and many others was at an all-time high. The demand for larger and more efficient machines opened the door for foreign companies such as O&K and Komatsu to firmly establish themselves in the United States as viable competitors. By the end of the 1970s, things were looking better for most consumers and heavy equipment manufactures alike. But disaster was right around the corner.

The sharp rise in interest rates in 1979 was the start of runaway inflation in the United States, and it led directly into the recession of 1980-1982. This had a profound effect on the manufacturing sector, and virtually every heavy equipment producer was affected. For companies such as Caterpillar, Bucyrus-Erie, P&H Harnischfeger, and Marion Power Shovel, 1982-1984 were some of the worst years on record. It wasn't until the mid- to late-1980s that these and other companies could spell the word "profit" with black ink again.

In the late 1980s and continuing into the 1990s, the best

9

survival method for many large equipment producers was to be part of a group of associated firms. For others, being merged into a larger organization was the only hope of survival. An example of such a company is the Terex Corporation, which includes Terex Americas, Terex Equipment Ltd., Clark Material Handling Co., Unit Rig, Koehring Cranes & Excavators, Northwest Engineering, BCP Construction Products, Fruehauf Trailer Corp., and Mark Industries. Another is INDRESCO, Inc., which includes the Jeffery Division, the Marion Division, and the Komatsu Dresser Company. This last company within INDRESCO handles the product lines of Komatsu, Dresser, Haulpak, and Galion.

Still another is the Volvo Construction Equipment Corp. (formerly known as VME), including Volvo BM, Michigan, Zettelmeyer, Akerman, and Euclid-Hitachi Heavy Equipment, Inc. Though AB Volvo does not own Hitachi, Hitachi does have a minority share in the Euclid hauler division. It is associations like these that give all those corporate lawyers something to do while confusing their customers to no end.

So far, the 1990s have not been the best of times for some of the giant machines working in the world. In the short period of 1990 to 1991, the world's largest shovel, dragline, and hauler were all retired. Between 1992 and 1994, six more active stripping shovels were parked or scrapped. That leaves only five still in operation, all in the United States. It is especially sad to see the massive stripping shovels going the way of the dinosaurs, since these machines are the end result of those childhood stories about steam shovels that were read to so many of us at bed time. Perhaps the images contained within these pages will make us remember their glory days and give us a new awareness of the histories that today's giants will someday leave behind.

The author, who stands 6ft, 4in in height, looks incredibly small next to the massive crawlers of the Marion 6360 stripping shovel. The tallest point on the crawler is a little over 16ft high, with a length of 45ft. Each of the track pads weighs 3.5 tons apiece and there are 42 of them per crawler belt.

CHAPTER 1

The Loading Shovels

TODAY'S MASSIVE LOADING SHOVELS CAN trace their ancestral roots directly to a small steam-powered shovel designed by William S. Otis in 1835 (for which he was granted a patent in 1839). Since then, there have been many manufacturers of shovels, including Lorain, Northwest, Lima, Insley, Link-Belt, Ransomes & Rapier, and Priestman, to name but a few. These firms all built great machines in their own right, but the three American-based companies of Bucyrus-Erie, Marion Power Shovel, and P&H Harnischfeger, produced the majority of all the large mining shovels used throughout the world.

The Bucyrus-Erie Company was established in 1880 as the Bucyrus Foundry & Manufacturing Co., in Bucyrus, Ohio, where they produced their first shovel, the "Thompson", in 1882. The company moved in 1893 to a new plant in South Milwaukee, Wisconsin, and in 1927, it merged with the Erie Steam Shovel Co., formerly known as the Ball Engine Co. The result was the Bucyrus-Erie Co., the name by which the company is known today.

To expand its worldwide sales, Bucyrus-Erie merged in 1930 with Ruston & Hornsby, Ltd., of England to form the overseas firm of Ruston-Bucyrus, Ltd. This firm's principal function was to handle sales of machines in Europe and represent the company in all overseas transactions.

Marion 301-M
In March 1991, the first Marion 301-M shovel to be commissioned in the United States started operations at the AMAX Belle Ayr mine in Wyoming's Powder River Basin (PRB) coal area. Equipped with a 54cu-yd dipper, rated at 80tons capacity, the shovel easily loads the mine's Unit Rig Lectra Haul MT-4000, 240ton capacity haulers in only three passes. A second Marion 301-M for AMAX, went to work a few months later at its Eagle Butte mine, also in the PRB. It was equipped with a 46cu-yd dipper, matched to the mine's current fleet of 190ton capacity haulers. The 301-M will remain Marion's largest shovel until its new 351-M, 85cu-yd, long-range coal-loading shovel is delivered at the end of 1995 to the PRB region of Wyoming. *Marion INDRESCO*

Marion 291-M

In 1963, Marion would again up the ante in the crawler shovel market with its 291-M. Once again, it was the largest two-crawler shovel the industry had ever seen. Two units were ordered by Peabody Coal Company for its Sinclair and Lynnville Mines. Both of these were delivered as long-range shovels with 15cu-yd dippers and extended 90ft boom lengths. Weight of the 291-M was 2,110,000lb (1,055ton). A standard range model of the 291-M was also conceived, with a 25cu-yd bucket on a 65ft boom, but none were ever manufactured. Today, both of the 291-Ms are currently working out West in the Powder River Basin at Powder River Coal Company's Rochelle Mine in Wyoming. The shovels have received a complete make-over, including larger 36 and 40cu-yd capacity coal loading buckets. *Marion INDRESCO*

Marion 191-M

The Marion Power Shovel Company of Marion, Ohio, introduced its first 191-M series shovel in 1951. At that time, it was the largest diesel-powered quarry and mining shovel on two crawlers. Equipped with 10 or 11cu-yd dippers, the first three units were delivered to Western Contracting Company for use on its many dam construction projects. Pictured in 1958 is Western's electric-powered Marion 191-M, loading a Euclid 1LLD 50ton hauler. Both units are painted in Western's distinctive orange color paint scheme.

Marion 201-M

Introduced around 1974, the Marion 201-M has bucket capacities ranging from 18 to 40cu-yds. Standard boom length is 51ft 6in. Average operating weight of the 201-M is 1,500,000lb (750ton). Pictured in 1979 is a 201-M loading a Unit Rig Lectra Haul M-120, rated at 120tons capacity. *Marion INDRESCO*

Marion 201-M
Shown here is the first of the upgraded Marion 201-M mining shovels, delivered in 1989 to Rossing Uranium Ltd., in Namibia, South Africa. The second unit, equipped with a 24cu-yd dipper, was delivered in February 1990 to the same mine. These machines incorporated many of the new features found on its bigger brother, the Marion 301-M. *Marion INDRESCO*

Some of Bucyrus-Erie's contributions to the industry included the first electric excavator in 1894, the first shovel mounted on crawlers in 1912, and the introduction of the first heavy duty, full revolving mining shovel, the 120-B, in 1925.

Marion, the chief rival of Bucyrus-Erie, was established in 1884, as the Marion Steam Shovel Co., and was located in Marion, Ohio. The early Marion shovels went by the name of "Barnhart's Steam Shovel and Wrecking Car". In 1921, Marion introduced its first intermediate-sized shovel, the Model 37, designed for the demanding digging conditions of quarries and mines. This and other smaller capacity machines led to

Marion 301-M
Introduced in July 1986, it was the largest two-crawler shovel that Marion had ever produced, the 301-M. Originally designed to accept bucket capacities in the 25-65cu-yd range, current machines now have increased load ranges with 32-85cu-yd ratings. Pictured here is the first prototype 301-M operating in Western Australia's Pilbara iron ore range at the Mt. Newman Mine. The shovel is currently equipped with a 36cu-yd capacity dipper rated at 70tons, specially suited for the high-density material in which the machine is working. The fairing on top of the operator's cab never made it past the pilot machine. The name on the boom, Dresser, was the parent company of Marion at the time of the 301-M's introduction. Marion is now a division of INDRESCO Inc. A second 301-M was commissioned at the same mine in March 1989. *Marion INDRESCO*

Marion 301-M
A Marion 301-M loads a 240ton capacity Haulpak 830E hauler in October 1990 for Newlands Coal Pty. Ltd., in Queensland, Australia. The 301-M shovel was designed to load these types of trucks in three passes with its 80-85ton capacity bucket. This unit has a boom length of 60ft and a crawler length of 37ft 6in. Height to the top of the point sheave, the tallest point on the shovel, is 61ft 8in. Full operating weight of the shovel is 2,300,000lb (1,150ton). *Marion INDRESCO*

the development of larger Marion shovels, such as the Model 4161 in 1935, the 151-M in 1945, and the famous 191-M in 1951.

In 1955, Marion purchased the Osgood Company, also located in Marion, Ohio, a company well known for its smaller

shovels. This was initiated by Marion to broaden its product line with excavators that appealed to smaller contractors.

The third major producer of mining shovels is the Harnischfeger Corporation, also known as P&H, located in West Milwaukee, Wisconsin. The company started in 1884 as the firm of Pawling & Harnischfeger, Engineers and Machinists. Though in its early years the company had more to do with sewing machine parts than shovels, it soon evolved into a manufacturer of overhead cranes. This led to the development of their bucket-wheel trencher excavators. P&H did not release its first electric mining shovel, the 1400 series, until 1944, and it was eventually followed by the 1600 series machines.

And it was with the first 25-cubic-yard (cu-yd) 2800 series

Marion 204-M Superfront
In 1979, Marion delivered the first two US-produced 204-M Superfront shovels. Pictured is the one unit delivered to Energy Fuels Mine, Energy, Colorado. It was equipped with a 30cu-yd dipper and cable-crowd, replacing the previous hydraulic set-up. In 1989, this same shovel was sold to Ulan Coal Mines Ltd. and shipped to Australia for use in its New South Wales coal operations. Average operating weight of the 204-M is 1,550,000lb (775ton). The 204-M has a capacity range of 20-45cu-yds, with a maximum 50ft digging height. The Superfront is still the only shovel on the market equipped with a variable-pitch dipper for a better fill factor of the bucket. *Marion INDRESCO*

Marion 204-M Superfront
With its unique front-end geometry, the Marion 204-M Superfront looks like no other shovel available. Sometimes looking monstrously complicated, the machine is actually based on well-established and proven design concepts. The end result is a shovel with increased capacity, lower overall weight, and better center of gravity. The Superfront model was announced by Marion in 1974, with the first units delivered to Russia in 1976. These machines were built under license by Sumitomo Heavy Industries in Japan. The Russians received a total of ten Superfronts over the next five years. The early Russian machines were equipped with hydraulic-crowd, as opposed to cable, to apply force to the bucket's digging action. Shown here in 1978 is one of the early 26cu-yd Marion/Sumitomo Superfronts loading a 2250fhp Unit Rig Lectra Haul M-200 in eastern Siberia, Russia. *Marion INDRESCO*

P&H 2800

In 1969, Harnischfeger Corporation, better known as P&H, delivered their first four 2800 series loading shovels to the Kaiser Resources Ltd. Balmer Mine, near Sparwood, British Columbia, Canada. With their 25cu-yd capacity dippers, they would lay claim to the title of the world's largest loading shovels. The early P&H 2800s weighed in at 1,811,000lb (906tons) and had a maximum 51ft 6in digging height. The boom length was 51ft. These early machines were also the first to be installed with P&H's Electrotorque system for converting AC electrical input into DC operating power. Pictured working here is one of the first four units loading a Unit Rig Lectra Haul M-200 hauler. This was also the first fleet of 200ton capacity haulers Unit Rig had put into service. *Harnischfeger Corp.*

shovels of 1969 that established P&H as a producer of ultra-large mining shovels, a tradition it proudly continues today.

Like the automotive rivalry between the "big three" of General Motors, Ford, and Chrysler, the competition of the mining industry's "big three" of Bucyrus-Erie, Marion, and P&H, has resulted in some of the most reliable and largest-capacity machines the world has ever known. It's likely that these three companies will be pushing each other right into the next century.

Left
P&H 2800
Though the 25cu-yd P&H 2800 may not have had the bulk of the Marion 291-M at the time, it did have a larger bucket capacity. Even though Marion had proposed 291-M shovels equipped with 33cu-yd dippers in the late 1960s, Kaiser felt that these machines were just too large for their current operations. Today, all four P&H 2800 shovels have worked over 100,000hr each and have received many upgrades over the years, including improved dippers and cabs. Here, a P&H 2800 is loading the world's largest dump truck, the 350ton capacity Terex 33-19 Titan hauler (in 1979), which also made its home at the Balmer Mine in British Columbia.

P&H 2800XPB
Over the years, the P&H 2800 series of shovels has included some of the most productive and reliable machines in the world. Upgraded versions include the 2800XP and 2800XPA models. The latest version of P&H's best-selling large shovel is the 2800XPB. This machine has many design improvements and upgrades over its predecessor. Most noticeable is the newly offset cab, giving the operator a better view while loading. Weight of the "XPB" model was now up to 2,220,000lb (1,110ton). Bucket capacity range is 33-70cu-yd, with a nominal capacity of 46cu-yd. Pictured is the second 2800XPB, equipped with a 40cu-yd dipper, delivered in early 1993. The shovel is working in a hard rock application, loading a 240ton capacity Haulpak 830E hauler at a copper mine in Mexico. *Harnischfeger Corp.*

Upper left

P&H 4100

In July 1991, Harnischfeger introduced its latest large-capacity shovel series, the P&H 4100. Delivered to Carter Mining Company's Caballo Mine, in Gillette, Wyoming, the first unit was equipped with a 59cu-yd/85ton capacity dipper. This enables the 4100 to load 240ton trucks in only three passes. Operating weight is 2,375,000lb (1,188 ton). Boom length is 60ft, with a maximum digging height of 55ft 7in. Today, the Caballo Mine is operated by Powder River Coal Company. *Harnischfeger Corp.*

Lower left

P&H 4100

One can never accuse Harnischfeger of resting on their laurels for too long. The P&H 4100 has already received some improvement upgrades since its introduction in 1991. The 4100 now comes with an offset cab, such as this 55cu-yd machine working in Indonesia, loading a Cat 793B, 240ton hauler. Weight on the most recent machines had also increased to 2,509,000lb (1,255ton). *Doug Walker*

P&H 4100

A large P&H 4100 takes a big bite with its 59cu-yd dipper at Boliden Mineral's Apirsa zinc mine in Aznalcollar, Spain, in 1992. *Harnischfeger Corp.*

P&H 5700LR

The world's largest two-crawler shovel series, the P&H 5700, was introduced in 1978. The first model produced was a 5700LR, long-range shovel, with a 25cu-yd capacity dipper on a 90ft boom length. Operating weight of the 5700LR was 3,674,000lb (1,837ton), and it is carried on crawlers with 45ft 7in lengths and 8ft 4in widths. The first and only 5700LR version was delivered to Arch of Illinois' Captain Mine and carried the nickname "Big Don". The shovel was moved to Arch of West Virginia in December 1991. Though shown in its red, white, and blue color scheme, the shovel was originally painted green.

24

P&H 5700
The second P&H 5700 produced was commissioned in June 1981 by
Bloomfield Collieries, for their Hunter Valley mine in Australia. This
was the first standard range version of the 5700, and it was equipped
with a 70ft boom. Dipper capacity for this unit is 60cu-yd and has a
maximum digging height of 63ft. *Harnischfeger Corp.*

P&H 5700XPA

The P&H 5700XPA is the latest and biggest version of the company's ultra-large electric shovel. The first of the 5700XPA shovels was erected at R.W. Miller & Company Pty Limited's Mount Thorley Mine in Queensland, Australia, in late 1990, and it was officially commissioned in January 1991. A second unit was also purchased by R.W. Miller's parent company, Coal and Allied Industries, for their Hunter Valley mine. It started work in July 1991. Both units carry 57.5cu-yd dippers and weigh in at 4,200,000lb (2,100ton) each. Pictured is the first unit as it gets ready to take its first bite "down under." *Harnischfeger Corp.*

P&H 5700XPA

The load range of the P&H 5700XPA is 60-90cu-yd, with a maximum 120ton load capacity. A total of five 5700 series shovels have been produced. Included in this number is the barge-mounted 5700 dredge "Chicago", owned by Great Lakes Dredge & Dock Company. The Chicago, as it was christened in 1987, can be equipped as a 28cu-yd dipper dredge, or as a 50cu-yd clamshell dredge. Pictured in 1991, is the first 5700XPA shovel, loading a 240ton capacity Dresser Haulpak 830E hauler. *Harnischfeger Corp.*

Bucyrus-Erie 295-BII
The Bucyrus-Erie 295-B series of electric mining shovels was introduced in 1972. Since then, they have been shipped all over the world, making them one of the most popular shovels in BE's product line. The 295-BII model was released about ten years later, with many design improvements and upgrades. Dipper capacity range is 22-45cu-yd, with a nominal 27cu-yd bucket. Average operating weight of the 295-BII shovel is 1,643,000lb (822ton). Boom length is 59ft, with a 57ft height clearance. *Bucyrus-Erie*

Bucyrus-Erie 395-B

When the 395-B shovel was released by Bucyrus-Erie in 1980, it was the first machine the company produced using its new ACUTROL AC motors, instead of the usual static DC type, to power the shovel. The first unit, nicknamed "Bruno", was delivered to Anamax Mining Company's Twin Buttes mine near Tucson, Arizona. Standard capacity was 34cu-yds, with a capacity range of 25 to 60cu-yds. Operating weight of the first machine was 1,831,000lb (916ton). *Bucyrus-Erie*

Bucyrus-Erie 395-BII

In 1991, BE released the updated version of their ACUTROL GTO drive system in the 395-BII shovel. This new AC system was a simplified, computerized version of the original one. The 395-BII class of shovel has a load range of 35-70cu-yds, with a nominal 44cu-yd dipper size. Boom length is 64ft. Weight of an average unit is 2,228,000lb (1114ton). *Bucyrus-Erie*

Bucyrus-Erie 495-B
The largest shovel currently produced by Bucyrus-Erie is the 495-B. Based on the proven 395-B series of BE machines, the 495-B is in the same class of shovels as the P&H 4100 and the Marion 301-M. Load capacity range of the 495-B is 40-80cu-yd, with a nominal 55cu-yd dipper. Operating weight of the shovel is 2,456,000lb (1,228ton). Pictured is the third machine manufactured, delivered to Hobet Mine No. 21, in southern West Virginia in February 1992. Equipped with a 52cu-yd capacity dipper, the shovel has no problem loading the mine's 240ton capacity Haulpak 830E haulers in only three passes.

CHAPTER 2

The Stripping Shovels

THE MOST POPULAR OF THE big shovels have been the incredible stripping machines produced for overburden removal in coal mining. Two companies alone, Bucyrus-Erie Co. and Marion Power Shovel Co., have been responsible for all of the gigantic super-stripping shovels ever produced. The development of these gigantic shovels paralleled development of smaller loading machines produced by these two manufacturers.

Marion has been credited with building the first strip mining shovel, the Model 250, in 1911, for Mission Mining near Oakwood, Illinois. Steam-powered and mounted on rails, it resembled the railroad-mounted shovels of the time, only larger. This Model 250 was equipped with a 3.5cu-yd dipper, which must have seemed large at the time but today could be matched by many excavators working along our interstates and freeways.

Marion produced the first electric stripping shovel, the Model 271, in 1915, and it was the first company to install crawlers on a stripping shovel, on its Model 350 in 1925.

One of the company's greatest achievements, however, was the building of the world's largest shovel, the monstrous 180cu-yd Marion 6360, produced for Southwestern Illinois Coal Corporation's Captain Mine in 1965. "The Captain", as it was named, was truly one of the great marvels of the earthmoving industry. To stand at its base and look straight up was almost guaranteed to take your breath away. Weighing more than 14,000 tons, it is in a class of mobile land machines that includes the BE 4250-W "Big Muskie" dragline and the

Bucyrus-Erie 1650-B
Pictured here in early 1962 is United Electric Coal Company's 70cu-yd capacity, 135ft-boomed Bucyrus-Erie 1650-B at its Fidelity Mine near Du Quoin, Illinois. The average weight of the later model 1650-B's was 5,747,000lb (2,874ton). After sitting idle for the last few years, this shovel was dismantled and scrapped in 1995. *Bucyrus-Erie*

Bucyrus-Erie 1650-B

Bucyrus-Erie released their first 1650-B stripping shovel in 1956. Christened the "River Queen", it was purchased by Peabody Coal Company for its River Queen mine, near Central City, Kentucky. The shovel was equipped with a 55cu-yd dipper on a 145ft boom and weighed in at 4,850,000lb (2,425ton). After some years of work, Peabody had the machine moved to its Riverview Mine. The shovel was eventually purchased by Green Coal Company, of Kentucky. The old "River Queen" was barged up to Green's Henderson County Mine No. 1 and is currently working to this very day. The shovel is shown here in August 1993.

Bucyrus-Erie 1050-B

Bucyrus-Erie was always known for building outstanding stripping shovels. An early example of one of their more popular models was the 1050-B. The first machine was built in 1941 and continued production as BE's largest shovel until the release of the 1650-B series. Average dipper capacity for the 1050-B was 36cu-yd, with a 113ft boom length. Operating weight was right around 3,070,000lb (1,535ton). Pictured is Green Coal's 40cu-yd Bucyrus-Erie 1050-B at its Panther Mine, near Owensboro, Kentucky. Put into operation in 1959, it had just been retired from service in April 1993 and had been sitting for only two weeks when this picture was taken. The large tower in the rear houses the movable counterweight which counterbalanced the weight of the empty bucket when the machine was in motion. The shovel exists no more, having been scrapped by the end of 1993.

240,000-cubic-meter (cu-m) output bucket wheel excavators of Germany. It's a very exclusive family, indeed.

The Bucyrus-Erie Co. introduced its first stripping shovel, the 175-B, in 1912 and was the first manufacturer to use a counter-balanced hoist on this type of machine, on its 750-B in 1930. Other stripping shovels produced by the company that used this hoist method included its 550-B, 950-B, and 1050-B.

The largest shovel produced by Bucyrus-Erie was its 140cu-yd 3850-B "Lot 2" machine, produced in 1964 for Peabody Coal's River King Mine. Though not as massive as "The Captain", it was still large enough to make one stare in utter disbelief.

It's interesting to note that Bucyrus-Erie had made design proposals for bigger shovels than its 140cu-yd 3850-B machine. Three of these include the BE 3950-B, a 150cu-yd, 19,500,000lb (9,750 ton), knee-action crowd shovel design of 1965; the BE 4850-B, a 220cu-yd, 28,000,000lb (14,000 ton) shovel of 1963; and the monstrous BE 4950-B, a 250cu-yd shovel, also in 1963. The 4950-B would have been a real record breaker, having an estimated weight of 36,000,000lb (18,000 ton), supported by sixteen crawlers, four per corner. The estimated cost in 1963 dollars was $16,200,000, plus electrical

Bucyrus-Erie 1650-B

Another of Green Coal's BE 1650-B shovels, this time equipped with a 70cu-yd bucket, is pictured working at its Panther Mine, near Owensboro, Kentucky, in May 1993. Having operated since 1964, the shovel was parked in August 1994. A total of five machines were built and of these, Green Coal now owns four of them, though two are used strictly for parts for the other machines.

equipment. It was a staggering sum for the time, but sounds cheap today—relatively speaking, of course. Bucyrus-Erie made presentations of the 4950-B to both Peabody and Southwestern Illinois, but no orders were ever placed. None of these proposed BE designs were ever built.

A little-known fact concerning some of Marion's and Bucyrus-Erie's stripping shovels involved the knee-action crowd front end, introduced by Marion on the 5561 series in 1940. In the early 1960s, Hanna Coal (part of Consolidation Coal Company, or CONSOL), placed an order with Bucyrus-Erie for a large stripper. The order included the condition that the machine must employ the knee-action crowd, sometimes called the "grasshopper leg" front end. Since this was an exclu-

continued on page 43

Bucyrus-Erie 1850-B

Sometimes, machines take on a life all their own, as with Bucyrus-Erie's 1850-B stripping shovel, "Brutus". Named by the superintendent, Emil Sandeen, of Pittsburg & Midway Coal Mining Company's Mine 19 in Hallowell, Kansas, the shovel started operation in May 1963. With its 90cu-yd dipper, it would work in this area for the next eleven years, uncovering more than 9,000,000tons of coal. The 1850-B stood about 160ft in height and was equipped with a 150ft boom. The weight of the shovel was 11,000,000lb (5,500ton). Only one 1850-B stripping shovel was ever made. Total cost for the machine in 1963 dollars was $6.5 million. *Big Brutus, Inc.*

Bucyrus-Erie 1850-B

In April 1974, the Bucyrus-Erie 1850-B, "Brutus"—or "Big Brutus" as it is now called—ceased operation. For the next ten years, the shovel was idle and was ravaged by the elements. But in 1983, P&M Coal Co. donated the shovel and sixteen acres surrounding the machine to Big Brutus, Inc., a non-profit organization dedicated to the restoration of the historic shovel. After financial help from P&M and thousands of volunteer hours, Big Brutus, on July 13, 1985, was dedicated as a museum and memorial to the coal mining history of southeast Kansas. In September 1987, the American Society of Mechanical Engineers dedicated Big Brutus as a Regional Historic Mechanical Engineering Landmark. The shovel is located south of West Mineral, Kansas, and is open to the public. *P&M Coal Co.*

Bucyrus-Erie 3850-B

Peabody Coal Company was always a strong supporter of Bucyrus-Erie's mining shovels. In August 1962, Peabody put BE's first 3850-B stripping shovel to work at its Sinclair Mine in western Kentucky. With a 115cu-yd capacity bucket and a 18,000,000lb (9,000ton) working weight, it was the world's largest mobile land machine at the time. Nicknamed "Big Hog", the shovel stood twenty stories tall, with a 210ft boom. More than 300 railroad cars were required to ship components from BE's South Milwaukee plant to the erection site. It then took approximately eleven months to assemble the massive shovel. In 1985, Big Hog's working days came to an end. The machine was salvaged for its parts, to be used on its sister machine in Illinois. The shovel was then scrapped and buried.

Bucyrus-Erie 3850-B

The BE 3850-B traveled on four crawler assemblies with two track units each. Each crawler was 40ft in length and 8ft tall. The tracks were made up of 37 linked pads weighing two tons apiece. The shovel was kept level by four large hydraulic leveling jacks, one on each crawler unit. The jacking system alone required 4,500gal of hydraulic fluid to operate properly. The crawlers were later updated to an oscillating bogie type of design, as opposed to the original ridged type pictured.

Bucyrus-Erie 3850-B
On August 13, 1964, Bucyrus-Erie's second 3850-B first filled its
dipper at Peabody's River King Mine No. 6, near Freeburg, Illinois.
Often referred to as the "Lot-2" machine, this 3850-B was the largest
stripping shovel Bucyrus-Erie ever made. The big shovel had a 140cu-
yd capacity dipper, as compared to 115cu-yd, for the "Lot-1" 3850-
B unit, at Peabody's Sinclair Mine. At 200ft, the boom length was
shorter on this machine than the first machine's 210ft. Weight of the
140cu-yd machine was 18,700,000lb (9,350ton). The shovel is
shown working in 1991. *David Stein*

Next page
Bucyrus-Erie 3850-B
The operator sat five stories above the ground, in an air-conditioned
cab, with a small galley off to one side. The front viewing area
protecting the operator is aviation-grade, shatterproof glass that is
almost an inch thick. The shovel is controlled by two hand levers and
two foot pedals. The 3850-B can accelerate from 0-25mph in eight
seconds, in a swing motion, and decelerate to a stop in four seconds.

Bucyrus-Erie 3850-B
The River King shovel knew only one day shift operator, a man by the name of Jim Pagliai. He took the very first scoop of earth with this shovel in 1964 and was on this machine during its last operating days in September 1992. The mighty "Lot-2" shovel was scrapped in 1993. During the machine's operational life, over 731,000,000cu-yds of overburden covering rich coal seams were removed. The image, taken in May 1992, shows the 3850-B working near Sparta, Illinois, about twenty miles from were the shovel originally started operations.

Bucyrus-Erie 3850-B
More than 210tons of overburden goes crashing into the pit's spoil pile from the 3850-B's 140cu-yd dipper. With the shovel being completely electrically powered, this dumping of overburden is about the loudest sound an observer will hear; the machine itself makes very little noise. Only the air-circulating fans are heard when the shovel swings its backside around. The bucket is attached to a 7ft diameter, 3in thick, hollow dipper handle. This allowed maintenance access to the interior of the handle to check for stress cracks. The entire structure is held by the saddle-block, which is mounted on the boom. The saddle-block alone weighs over 200tons. The dipper handle's working range is 125ft, with a 180ft overall length. For size comparison, note the mechanic in the white T-shirt, on the boom, by the dipper handle.

Bucyrus-Erie 3850-B

The massive 140cu-yd bucket of the Bucyrus-Erie 3850-B "Lot-2" shovel, at Peabody's River King Mine, has a dipper capacity of over 210tons. But under varying heaped load conditions, it could hold as much as 148cu-yd, or 220tons. The bucket has received many additional steel welding reinforcements over its twenty-year life span. Here, a welder is preparing to fix a shim on one of the bucket caps that has worked loose.

Bucyrus-Erie 1950-B

Bucyrus-Erie's 1950-B—"The GEM of Egypt"—stripping shovel was the second-largest-capacity shovel the company ever produced. It was equipped with a 130cu-yd dipper that had a capacity of almost 200tons. The "GEM" was the second shovel BE designed with a knee-action crowd front end. The first machine was BE's 1950-B "Silver Spade". The word "GEM" in the shovel's name stands for "Giant Excavating Machine," and "Egypt" stood for the mine in which the shovel started working: the Egypt Valley Mine of Hanna Coal Company, in Barnesville, Ohio. Its first full month of operation was February 1967. The GEM is shown in its original white and red Hanna color paint scheme. By the mid-1970s, the shovel was repainted yellow and orange, the new corporate colors of Consolidation Coal Company (CONSOL), of which Hanna was a part. *Bucyrus-Erie*

Bucyrus-Erie 1950-B

The GEM of Egypt had its first public exposure at a special open house on January 21 and 22, 1967, for all the residents of the Cadiz and Barnesville, Ohio, area. It was very common for mining companies to show off their latest Goliaths as a goodwill gesture toward the public. Of course today, this is all but unthinkable to let the public this close to a machine on mine property. With the amount of frivolous lawsuits issued today, a stubbed toe could now cost you millions. *Dale Davis Collection*

Bucyrus-Erie 1950-B

Mine areas can be very dangerous at times. Without warning in 1976, part of the highwall peeled away and collapsed on The GEM, causing about $1 million in damages. Luckily, no one was seriously hurt. The name of the shovel by this time had also been shortened, since it was no longer working at the Egypt Valley Mine site. Repairs were made, and the shovel continued to work until the mine temporarily shut down, from May 1985 through 1986. The 1950-B once again started back to work in 1987, only to be parked in August 1988. *Dale Davis Collection*

Bucyrus-Erie 1950-B

Consolidation Coal Company's (CONSOL) first Bucyrus-Erie 1950-B stripping shovel was "The Silver Spade", which started working in November 1965. The name commemorates the 25th anniversary of the Hanna Coal Company, a division of the CONSOL group. It was the first stripper on which Bucyrus-Erie utilized the knee-action crowd front end design, which helped eliminate all torsional and bending stresses from the main boom. This allowed the machine's boom to be of a lighter construction than the earlier, two-piece BE designs. The Spade is shown operating at Mahoning Valley Mine No. 36, in Cadiz, Ohio, in May 1994.

Bucyrus-Erie 1950-B

Starting in late 1991, The GEM fell victim to the scrapper's cutting torches, and by early 1992, the job was complete. The shovel was just not worth the cost of moving it to a new mining location six miles away. It ended its working days at Mahoning Valley Mine No. 33, in Cadiz, Ohio. In its working lifetime, the shovel moved approximately 548,222,376cu-yd of earth. The 1950-B GEM was equipped with a 170ft boom and stood 178ft tall. Total operating weight of the shovel was 14,000,000lb (7,000ton). The mighty GEM is pictured kicking up a little dust only a few months before she would be parked for the last time. *David Stein*

sive feature of Marion's, a "quiet" agreement was reached between the two companies. Bucyrus-Erie could use the knee-action front end, utilizing Marion's one-piece boom design. In return, Marion would get the use of Bucyrus-Erie's cable crowd design, to be used instead of its own rack-and-pinion system.

In the end, Hanna got its shovel, the BE 1950-B "Silver Spade", and it put in an order for a second of the same design, a machine which became "The GEM of Egypt". These were the only two shovels by Bucyrus to utilize the special front end. Marion, on the other hand, utilized the cable-crowd concept on some of its 5761 shovels and all of its 5900 and 5960 series strippers.

The time of the giant stripping shovel is almost at an end. With only five machines currently at work, all in the United States, their years of operation are numbered. Only one of the shut-down machines has been turned into a museum while all the others have either been cut up or are waiting for their turn to be scrapped. These mechanical giants are literally going the way of the dinosaurs, to extinction.

Bucyrus-Erie 1950-B

"The Spade" stands 220ft tall and is equipped with a boom 200ft in length, as compared to the GEM's 170ft version. It also had a longer dipper handle of 122ft compared to the GEM's 102ft handle. This allowed the Spade to have a greater working range and operate in deeper digging conditions than the GEM.

Bucyrus-Erie 1950-B

The bucket capacity of the Bucyrus-Erie 1950-B Silver Spade is rated at 105cu-yd, with an approximate 160ton load limit. This was smaller than its sister shovel, the 1950-B GEM, which was rated at 130cu-yd.

Right
Bucyrus-Erie 1950-B

The Silver Spade started life painted in the Hanna Coal Company's white and red color scheme. But before the new CONSOL paint job was finished, the shovel was idled on October 1, 1982. It would spend the next six years sitting in the pit were it had last worked. The decision was made to resurrect the Spade, though at the cost of its sister machine, the GEM. Parts removed from the GEM were used in the restoration of the other shovel, and on April 8, 1989, the Spade returned to service. It is currently scheduled to work until the end of the decade, unless some unforeseen mechanical mishap or financial fluctuations in the coal market make it uneconomical to operate.

Bucyrus-Erie 1950-B
Like all major stripping shovels, the Bucyrus-Erie 1950-B Silver Spade rides on four crawler sets. Each crawler-track is 34ft long and 8ft high. Pictured here is the newer design of the tracks. The earlier versions used a finer, multi-link pad design, and they were constantly breaking. As these tracks wore out, they were replaced with the updated pad versions. The crawlers on the Spade were of the same design as that of the GEM. In fact, one set, saved from the scrapped GEM, was used recently to replace one of the Spade's units. The shovels travel movement is controlled by the ground crew, from a lower platform between the crawler sets, not from the operator's cab. The weight carried by the huge crawlers of both 1950-Bs was the same: 14,000,000lb (7,000ton).

Marion 5561
The Marion 5561 series of stripping shovels were the first equipped with the knee-action crowd front end. These machines replaced the previous 5560 series that last used the counter-balanced hoist method similar to that employed in Bucyrus-Erie's large strippers of the time. The average bucket capacity of the 5561 was 40cu-yd, and it had a working weight of 3,575,000lb (1,788ton). Pictured working in 1980 at Peabody Coal's Power Mine near Montrose, Missouri, is a 5561 built in 1942. As often happens with machines that are of this vintage, it was scrapped when this mine closed in 1987. In its production run from 1940 to 1956, a total of seventeen 5561 shovels were produced. *Keith Haddock*

47

Left
Marion 5760
Probably one of the most famous shovels of all time, and the first of the so called "super-strippers", was the Marion 5760 "Mountaineer". When it went to work in eastern Ohio in January 1956, it was the largest mobile land machine ever produced. The Mountaineer was owned by the Hanna Coal Company, a division of the CONSOL group of coal companies. Four sets of crawlers carried the machine's weight of 5,500,000lb (2,750ton). Each of the eight track sections was 23ft long and 7ft high. The overall height of the shovel was 147ft to the top of the boom point, and it was equipped with a 65cu-yd dipper on a 150ft boom. Pictured is the shovel as it gets ready to leave its assembly area in December 1955. *Consolidation Coal Co.*

Marion 5760
The Marion 5760 "Mountaineer" was one of five 5760 stripping shovels produced by the Marion Power Shovel Company. The Mountaineer introduced many new features to the shovels of the day, including a centrally located elevator. The big shovel came equipped with dual cabs, so the operator had a clear view, no matter the direction in which the shovel was digging. The Mountaineer operated with two different bucket configurations, a round bottom and a flat bottom version. The round bottom was the preferred choice. Capacity of both dippers was 65cu-yds. Early specifications listed the capacity at 60cu-yd, but this was for internal company purposes only. The Mountaineer would work for the next twenty-three years, until being parked in January 1979. For the next nine years, the once-proud shovel endured the elements and the graffiti and damage caused by vandals. The machine that once made newspaper headlines all over the world in the 1950s was finally put out of its misery and scrapped in late 1988.

Marion 5761

The most popular model line of super-stripping shovels produced by any manufacturer was the Marion 5761 series, introduced in 1959. Nineteen of these shovels went into service, with most of them going into Kentucky, Illinois, and Indiana coal mines, though one shovel did find its way down to Alabama. Pictured working in 1977, at Peabody Coal Company's Lynnville Mine in Indiana, is the mighty "Stripmaster". This 5761 was erected in 1959 and was equipped with a 65cu-yd dipper, on a 165ft boom. Today, the shovel is no longer in regular operation but is kept on standby should the mine ever need to increase its production capacity. *Marion INDRESCO*

Left
Marion 5760

Another of Marion's five 5760 stripping shovels was Peabody Coal Company's "Big Paul, the King of Spades", which operated at the River King Mine near Freeburg, Illinois. Pictured working in 1958, it was equipped with a 70cu-yd dipper, as compared to the original 5760 Mountaineer, which used a 65cu-yd bucket.

Marion 5761
Pictured is a Marion 5761, with standard rack-and-pinion crowd, working at the AMAX Sun Spot Mine in Vermont, Illinois, in June 1978. This 5761 was equipped with a 65cu-yd dipper, on a 170ft boom. Operating weight of this version was 7,575,000lb (3,788ton). The Sun Spot Mine opened in November 1962 and ceased operations in December 1983. *Marion INDRESCO*

Left
Marion 5761
This Marion 5761 started operations in 1964 at the Captain Mine of Southwestern Illinois Coal, now Arch of Illinois. It had a taller gantry and an elevated cab for stripping two coal seams at once. It carried a 60cu-yd dipper on a 190ft boom. This shovel worked at Arch Minerals' Horse Creek Mine for the last several years before it was idled in August 1994. *Arch of Illinois, Inc.*

Marion 5761

Another Marion 5761 stripping shovel, this time operating at Consolidation Coal Company's (CONSOL) Burning Star No. 2 mine, near Du Quoin, Illinois, in May 1993. This machine started working in August 1961, for the Truax Traer Coal Co., carrying the name "Big Dipper". In 1962, Truax Traer became part of the CONSOL group of coal companies. The shovel was originally white and red, and when it was repainted in the 1970s, the name of the machine was painted over. It carried a 65cu-yd dipper on a 170ft for its entire working life.

Marion 5761

Each of the CONSOL's Marion 5761 shovel's eight crawler sections is 23ft long, 5ft wide, 8ft high and weigh 83,000lb apiece. Total weight carried by these is 6,562,000lb (3,281ton). With its working days having ended, the last of the operating 5761 shovels was retired in November 1994.

Right
Marion 5860

Marion produced only two of its 5860 series stripping shovels. The first machine started operation in June 1965, at CONSOL's Truax Traer Coal Company's Red Ember mine, near Fiatt, Illinois. Both 5860s had 80cu-yd dippers and 180ft booms. The working weight of each shovel was 10,150,000lb (5,075ton). A 5861 series of shovels was proposed by Marion, but none were ever built. The first 5860 shovel, pictured here, has since been scrapped.

Marion 5860
The second Marion 5860 shovel started work in 1966, at Truax Traer's Burning Star No. 3 mine, near Sparta, Illinois. After the shovel was retired by CONSOL, it was sold in the early 1980s to Arch of Illinois, for use at its Captain Mine. The shovel was converted into a bucket wheel excavator, called the 5872WX, to work in conjunction with Arch's 180cu-yd Marion 6360 shovel. *Marion INDRESCO*

Right
Marion 5860
The 80cu-yd dipper of the second Marion 5860 comfortably cradles a large Caterpillar dozer in 1966. The bucket alone weighs 81 tons. Its inside dimensions are 11ft, top to bottom; 12ft 6in, front to back; and 14ft wide.

Marion 5960

The 5960 was the second-largest shovel that Marion had ever manufactured. With its 125cu-yd capacity dipper on a 215ft boom, it ranked as the fourth-largest shovel in the world. The 5960 weighed in at 18,000,000lb (9,000ton), carried on eight crawler units that were 40ft long and 8ft wide. The shovel was delivered in 1969, to Peabody Coal Company's River Queen Mine, in Greenville, Kentucky, and it carried the name of the "Big Digger". In 1988, operations were suspended at the River Queen Mine. The mine was officially shut down in 1989, and the shovel was dismantled at the end of that year. Only one Marion 5960 was ever built. *Marion INDRESCO*

Marion 5900

Marion delivered their first 5900 series stripping shovel to Peabody Coal Company's Lynnville Mine, located in Lynnville, Indiana. The shovel was put into service in November 1968 and was equipped with a 105cu-yd dipper. Boom length was 200ft, and the entire machine weighed in at 14,500,000lb (7,250ton). Each of the eight sections of crawlers is 34ft in length. The 5900 is pictured in 1977, with its original Peabody colors. It has since been repainted in the company's updated colors of bright yellow for the upper portion, including the gantry, and green for the lower section. All lettering and logos were removed during the repaint. *Marion INDRESCO*

Marion 5900

The Marion 5900, at Peabody's Lynnville Mine, takes a big 160ton-plus bite of overburden in its 105cu-yd dipper. At times, it seems the rocks literally explode from the massive pressure exerted by the cutting edges of the bucket. *Marion INDRESCO*

Right
Marion 5900

The Marion 5900 shovel that was delivered to the AMAX Coal Company's Leahy Mine, in southern Illinois, was the last of the super-strippers, not only from Marion but from any manufacturer. This was the second 5900 produced by Marion, but it was one of the most advanced for the breed. The shovel started working in October 1971 and was equipped with the industry's first variable-pitch dipper design. This allowed for better control of the bucket while uncovering two seams of coal at the same time. This unit had a taller gantry than the first 5900 built, and a 210ft boom. This allowed for better dipper placement for removing the overburden from the upper seam of coal. Capacity of the bucket was 105cu-yd. The shovel was purchased, along with the rest of the Leahy Mine, by Arch of Illinois, in March 1986, for use at its Captain Mine. In August 1992, the shovel received its new Arch white-and-blue color scheme. The 5900 will work as long as there is a need for coal from the Captain Mine. The shovel is shown in its original AMAX colors in June 1984. *AMAX Coal Co.*

Marion 5900

Shown here is the Marion 5900's 105cu-yd, 160ton capacity, variable-pitch control bucket, now working at Arch of Illinois' Captain Mine. Notice the hinged design of the dipper and the stops, at the front and rear, that enable the bucket to rotate under load. This allows it to work flat on the pit floor and provides a better cutting action on the face of the high wall. The first 5900, delivered to the Peabody Lynnville Mine, was later retrofitted with this type of dipper design.

Left
Marion 6360
The largest shovel ever produced, of any kind, was the incredible 180cu-yd capacity Marion 6360. Purchased by Southwestern Illinois Coal Corporation, it was the crown jewel at their Captain Mine, near Percy, Illinois. The 6360 was designed to uncover two seams of coal simultaneously. It first would remove the overburden from the upper seam of coal, next to the shovel. This would then make room for the removal of the parting, the material between the two seams of coal, directly in front of the shovel. The 6360 was officially dedicated on October 15, 1965. Pictured is "The Captain", as it was christened, in its original Southwestern colors and bucket design. The dipper would under go increased strengthening modifications in the years to come. Total cost of the shovel in 1965 was $15 million.

Marion 6360
The Marion 6360 became the world's largest mobile land machine when it was introduced in 1965, weighing in at 28,000,000lb (14,000ton). Towering twenty-one stories in the air, everything about this machine was huge. The housing alone was 88ft wide. The main boom was 215ft in length and came equipped with a 133ft dipper handle. Unique to the 6360 was the dual gantry design for the rack-and-pinion driven crowd. The shovel had a 16ft height clearance between the crawler assemblies, so equipment could safely pass underneath it during operation. Pictured is the 6360 in 1984, wearing the colors of Arch Mineral Corporation, the new owners of the Captain Mine. Missing is "The Captain", the nickname that was painted on the back side of the machine. For whatever reason, the name of the shovel was never put back on. *Keith Haddock*

Marion 6360

Maintenance crews would swing into action whenever the shovel was shut down. Whether for repairs, or to take on supplies, there was always work to be done on such a mammoth machine. Large cable reels at the front and rear supply power to the Marion 6360. By having two reels, the shovel never needs to turn around to change directions in the pit. *David Stein*

Marion 6360

The crawlers on the Marion 6360 were enormous by any standards. Each of the eight crawler sections was 45ft long, 10ft wide and 16ft high. Each track consisted of 42 pads, each weighing 3.5tons apiece. The shovel is shown being moved to a new pit location in early 1990. The large wooden pallets keep the machine on a level surface and from sinking into the ground. *Arch of Illinois, Inc.*

Marion 6360

On September 9, 1991, "The Captain" shovel was mortally wounded by a fire in its lower compartments. The blaze was extremely hard to contain because of the location of the machine and the build-up of grease and oil in the swing circle area. The fire was able to smolder and burn for some time before it was extinguished. After investigation, it was thought that a hydraulic line had burst and sprayed fluid over several live electrical panels in the lower compartments, causing the fire to ignite. Marion technicians were brought in to survey the damage and determined that the shovel could be repaired. But with cost estimates ranging over $2 million and no guarantee that the shovel would perform as before, the decision was made to scrap the 6360. Pictured in July 1992, the shovel stood proud until the very end. Demolition crews moved in at the end of 1992 and scrapped the behemoth. All that remains of the shovel today is the US flag that was flying on it at the time of the fire. It is now proudly displayed in the lobby of Arch of Illinois' mine offices, in honor of the mightiest shovel of them all, the Marion 6360.

Marion 6360

The bucket on the Marion 6360 was the largest ever constructed for a shovel. It had a 180cu-yd capacity and an average 270ton load rating. The dipper alone weighed 330,000lb (165ton) empty! Also, this bucket was equipped with double doors, which helped reduce the shock impact when they closed after the load had been dumped. The mouth of the dipper was 18ft 6in wide, 16ft high and 24ft 6in deep. In its lifetime, this bucket was responsible for the removal of over 809,300,000cu-yd of overburden at the Captain Mine. *David Stein*

Earthmoving Equipment Helps
Launch Rockets

Located at the John F. Kennedy Space Center (KSC) in Florida are two massive land vehicles that have played a very important part in man's exploration of space. Though they are not considered "earthmoving" machines by any stretch of the imagination, they are based on such machines nonetheless.

In 1961, NASA needed some type of mobile transporter to take the Saturn V vehicle from its protective building to its launch pad. After more than a year of study, an internal report was submitted by Donald D. Buchanan, then chief of the Launcher Systems and Umbilical Tower Design Section, and an associate, G. W. Walter, on June 11, 1962. The report looked at three types of systems—and their advantages and disadvantages—that might address the problem. Concepts that were considered included a barge and canal system, a rail system, and the land transporter. The report concluded that the crawler/transporter system would be the most reliable and cost-effective. On June 13, 1962, KSC management accepted the transporter concept, and NASA approved it the following month.

Two large equipment manufacturers, Bucyrus-Erie Co. and Marion Power Shovel Co., were approached to build the two crawler/transporters that NASA needed. In March 1963, Marion was awarded the contract to build both units, at a cost of $13,600,000.

Both of the Marion Crawler-Transporters were built in Ohio and assembled and tested on-site at the KSC during 1965 and early 1966. The transporters' designs were adapted from Marion's

Marion Crawler-Transporters
Pictured in January 1973 at the Kennedy Space Center's Complex 39 in Florida is one of the two Marion Crawler-Transporters as it prepares to pick up the mobile launcher used for the launch of Apollo 17. Each transporter is 131ft in length, 114ft in width and weighs in at 6,000,000lb (3,000ton), unloaded. Maximum payload capacity is approximately 12,500,000lb (6,250ton). *NASA*

Marion Crawler-Transporters

One of the transporters moves away from Launch Pad 39B after positioning the Space Shuttle Columbia atop the mobile launcher platform for Mission STS-40, in May 1991. Each of its crawler sections is 7ft 6in wide, 10ft tall, and 41ft 3in in length. The belt or track is made up of 57 cleats that weigh one ton apiece. *NASA*

mammoth stripping shovels, with the lower crawler sections serving as a guide for the transporters' base.

The massive crawler-transporters travel at just under 1 mph, with load, on its 3.5 mi trip to the launch pad. Top speed is 2mph, unloaded, on its return trip.

Propulsion for each unit is provided by two 2750hp diesel engines driving four 1000kW generators that deliver power to sixteen traction motors. A separate system consisting of two 1065hp diesel engines driving two 750kW generators supplies AC power for the load leveling, jacking, steering, ventilating, and electrical needs of the unit.

The crawler-transporters have performed their duties admirably, for both the Saturn and now the Space Shuttle programs. In 1977, both units were designated as National Historic Mechanical Engineering Landmarks by the American Society of Mechanical Engineers.

Also in 1977, extensive modifications and updates were performed on both units. This included the installation of a new central control room and a programmable rapid trouble-shooting diagnostics system. Also, a laser docking system was installed to help the driver dock the transporter at the launch pad.

On April 22, 1990, an important milestone was reached in the life of Crawler-Transporter No. 2. While transporting the Space Shuttle Columbia to the launch pad for the STS-35 mission in May, it passed the 1,000mi mark in service. At the time, Crawler-Transporter No. 1 was only 25mi behind, and it too has since exceeded the 1,000mi mark.

The largest load ever transported by one of the units was by unit No. 2, when it carried the Saturn 1B/Skylab vehicle on its mobile launcher platform. The total payload totaled 13.2 million pounds, more than twice the weight of the transporter itself.

The future of the space program, more than anything else, holds the key as to how long these giant land vehicles (nicknamed "Hans" and "Franz" after the popular "Saturday Night Live" characters) remain in operation. As long as the Space Shuttles keep flying, the crawlers will be needed to perform their duties.

CHAPTER 3

The Draglines

THE WALKING DRAGLINES OF TODAY are the largest single-bucket earthmoving machines currently in use around the world. These machines, along with environmental rule changes, brought the era of the stripping shovel to an end. Thus, it shouldn't be surprising that the three major manufacturers of these mammoth digging machines are also the leading suppliers of large electric mining shovels: Bucyrus-Erie Co., Marion Division of INDRESCO, Inc., and P&H Harnischfeger Corp.

The first practical dragline ever produced was equipped with a two-line bucket system. John W. Page of the Chicago-based firm of Page & Shnable is credited with building it in 1903. In 1907, Page started to buy specialized equipment for his draglines from the Monighan Machine Works, also located in Chicago. After the success of their first joint effort, an informal agreement was reached by the two firms in which the companies would help each other manufacture and sell their dragline creations. In 1913, Oscar J. Martinson of the Monighan Machine Corp. patented the first "walking" mechanism for dragline use, referred to as the "Martinson Tractor". It was installed on Monighan's first walking dragline that same year. Page continued to buy machinery from Monighan until about 1916, when the companies went their separate ways.

The Bucyrus-Erie Co. was interested in entering the dragline market. To save development costs, Bucyrus-Erie bought controlling interest in the Monighan firm, already firmly established in the production of draglines, in 1931. The joint venture was known as Bucyrus-Monighan. This arrangement worked out well for both companies, and in 1946, the

Bucyrus-Erie 3270-W (Lot-1)
At the end of 1979, Bucyrus-Erie put their first 3270-W dragline to work at AMAX's Delta Mine, in Marion, Illinois. Referred to as the "Lot-1" machine, the dragline was the second largest built by BE, just behind "Big Muskie." *Bucyrus-Erie*

Marion 8800

The first of the Marion 8000 series of draglines and the first to break the 100cu-yd barrier was the 8800. Marion received the order from Peabody Coal Company in 1961 for the 8800, for use at its Homestead Mine in Kentucky. It was over twice as large as its nearest competitor, carrying an 85cu-yd capacity bucket on a 275ft boom, which was later upgraded to a 100cu-yd version. Weight for the machine was 12,570,000lb (6,285ton), a staggering amount for the day, but one that would soon be eclipsed by even larger units. The 8800 is currently located at Peabody's Ken Mine, near Beaver Dam, Kentucky.

rest of the Monighan company was formally merged into the Bucyrus-Erie organization. This eventually led to the manufacture of one of the largest digging machines the world has ever known, the 220cu-yd BE 4250-W "Big Muskie" walking dragline, in 1969.

Marion Power Shovel Co. was well aware of the implications of Bucyrus-Erie, their chief rival, having a line of walking draglines while Marion had none. So Marion decided to design their own "walker," and in 1939 it released the first machine in its Model 7200 series. This was the start of a long production

run of some of the industry's finest machines. These include such draglines as the long-running Model 7400 and the large 8000 series of machines introduced in the early 1960s.

Even though Bucyrus-Erie can lay claim to the largest dragline ever made, Marion is not without its great achievements when it comes to these types of machines. The largest dragline produced by Marion was its 8950 series, rated at 150cu-yd, which was considerably smaller than the 220cu-yd BE machine. But in January 1994, Marion released two special Model 8750 units: A 104cu-yd machine went to Queensland, Australia, and the other, a 106cu-yd unit, was shipped to Alberta, Canada. What makes these draglines so special is that each of these 8750s is equipped with a 420ft boom, the largest ever built. This gives the machines an incredible range in any working situation. By comparison, this length is about twice as long as the largest stripping shovel boom ever produced.

Around 1987, P&H Harnischfeger did what Bucyrus-Erie did years earlier—enter the walking dragline business—by purchasing a well-established and respected manufacturer of the machines, Page Engineering Company, the early pioneer in

Marion 8900

In 1966, Marion introduced the 8900 series of draglines. Two such units were built and delivered in 1967. The first went to Thiess Peabody-Mitsui Coal Pty., Ltd., at its Moura Mine, in Queensland, Australia. This machine was equipped with a 130cu-yd bucket, on a 275ft boom. The second one was shipped to Peabody Coal Company's Dugger Mine, in southern Indiana. It was equipped with a 145cu-yd capacity bucket, on a 250ft boom, and had a total operating weight of 14,000,000lb (7,000ton). Today, this machine works at Peabody Coal's Hawthorn Mine in Indiana, and it was recently upgraded with a new 155cu-yd bucket in 1993.

dragline technology. The resulting machines were initially marketed as P&H/Page draglines, but after the first couple of years, the Page name was dropped entirely. P&H has continued the model numbers used by Page, including the Model 757, rated at 75cu-yd, the largest that the Page company ever built. (A Model 9100 machine with a 120cu-yd capacity was designed but never built.)

The first P&H dragline designed and built entirely in-house—and not based on an existing Page design—is the P&H 9020, currently under construction at Bulga Coal Management Limited's Bulga and Saxonvale open cut mines in eastern Australia's Hunter Valley. The machine will be equipped with 110cu-yd and 120cu-yd buckets on a 320ft boom and is scheduled to be commissioned sometime in early 1996.

Another producer of walking draglines over the years is the Ransomes & Rapier company of England, established in 1937. The Rapier machines were not as large as the American-made units, with the largest capacity machines in the 45 to 65cu-yd range. In the late 1980s, the Rapier model line was purchased by Bucyrus-Erie and marketed through the BE European company. To date, no new Rapier designs have been produced since the buyout.

The only other manufacturers of large draglines today are two Russian companies: Novokramatorsk Engineering Works

Marion 8750

In 1971, Marion introduced one of its most popular ranges of large-capacity draglines, the 8750. This series of machines has a capacity rating of 100-135cu-yd and a boom size range of 335-430ft. Maximum operating weight is 14,200,000lb (7,100ton). Pictured is an 8750, working at American Electric Power's (AEP) Central Ohio Coal Co., at its Muskingum mine, in August 1992. It is equipped with a 110cu-yd bucket on a 335ft boom. The housing alone is 109ft in length, with a 116ft width. Total operating weight of this machine is 13,100,000lb (6,550ton). The Central Ohio 8750 was originally purchased from AMAX Coal and started operation at the Muskingum mine in June 1980. Sad to say, this faithful Marion was parked at the end of 1994, after its reclamation duties were finished.

Marion 8750
At the same Australian Curragh mine as the 135cu-yd Marion 8750, is this 110cu-yd 8750 that started operations in 1986. Equipped with a 335ft boom, it had originally been built for a US company but was never put to work. As the small pick-up truck in the photo indicates, it doesn't matter what size the bucket is; all Marion 8750s are "big" machines! *Marion INDRESCO*

Left
Marion 8750
The largest 8750 series dragline that Marion has built so far was delivered to Curragh Queensland Mining Ltd., near Blackwater, Queensland, Australia, in December 1991. Equipped with a 135cu-yd bucket on a 360ft boom, it is currently the largest capacity dragline working in Australia. This machine was also the first dragline in the world equipped with Marion's patented planetary swing system. This system supplies more swing power required by larger capacity machines but takes up less space in the confines of existing dragline machinery housings. By the end of 1994, over twenty Marion 8750s had been sold worldwide. *Marion INDRESCO*

(NKMZ), producers of walking draglines and large cable shovels; and the Uralmashavod Heavy Engineering Works (UZTM), manufacturers of the ESh line of draglines, EKG cable mining shovels, and EG hydraulic shovels.

Large, two-crawler draglines are few in number compared to the giant walking machines, and only a few manufacturers build them. Among them: Manitowoc Engineering Co. produces its 6400 series, rated at 15cu-yd; American Crane Corp. offers its American 12220, rated at 10cu-yd; and P&H builds a single model, the 2355, rated at 20cu-yd. Marion has produced the most models of this type of dragline over the years, and they include the Marion 184-M, rated at 12cu-yd; the 195-M, rated at 17cu-yd; and the Marion 305-M, currently the world's largest, with a maximum load capacity of 24cu-yd.

Very few four-crawler draglines have been built by the industry. One of those was the Bucyrus-Erie 300-D, rated at 14cu-yd. The first unit of this model was commissioned in late

Marion 8950

The 150cu-yd bucket on the Marion 8950 was the largest ever originally installed by the manufacturer on any of its draglines. The size of this bucket was enormous. The only Marion dragline that has a larger capacity unit is the 8900 at the Peabody Hawthorn Mine. The original 145cu-yd bucket was replaced by a new 155cu-yd unit that was built by an outside supplier, Minserco, Inc., in 1993.

Marion 8950

The largest dragline ever produced by Marion was its 8950 model, equipped with a 150cu-yd capacity bucket, on a 310ft boom. Total operating weight of the machine was 14,600,000lb (7,300ton). The only 8950 ever built started work in October 1973, at the AMAX Ayrshire Mine, near Evansville, Indiana. Pictured is the Marion in July 1992.

Right
Marion 8950

The Marion 8950 at work in February 1978. Casting out over 225tons of earth and rock, the 8950 has a maximum allowable suspended load rating of 775,000lb, which includes the weight of the load and the complete bucket assembly. The Marion has a maximum digging depth of 160ft. In December 1993, the surface activities of AMAX's Ayrshire Mine ceased operations. With the removal of all of that mine's coal that was economical to mine, the Marion 8950 now works reclamation duties to restore the land to its original state. When this is completed, the dragline will be parked. Whether it finds a new home, or becomes fodder for the scrappers' cutting torches, only time will tell. *Marion INDRESCO*

Bucyrus-Erie 1550-W

For years, the Bucyrus-Erie 1550-W "Big Geordie" was the largest dragline operating in Europe. Equipped with a 65cu-yd capacity bucket, on a 265ft boom, Big Geordie was capable of digging to depths of 150ft. The big dragline started operations in August 1969, for Derek Crouch, at its Radar North mine, in the United Kingdom. From 1977 to 1991, the machine was in the control of Taylor Woodrow Ltd., working at its Butterwell site. By the end of 1991, most of the coal deposits had been removed and Big Geordie was shut down. One hopes, the 65cu-yd machine finds a new home sometime in the future. If not, it will meet with a very sad end indeed. *Bucyrus-Erie*

1979 by Downen Enterprises for its Harrisburg, Illinois, mine. Based on the BE 380-W walking dragline, it was marketed on the principle of its modular construction. Sad to say, few of these machines were ever sold.

Bucyrus-Erie 2570-W
A very popular line of large-capacity draglines for Bucyrus-Erie has been the 2570-W series, introduced in 1972. These machines were designed for loads exceeding 100cu-yds. Pictured is AEP's Central Ohio Coal Company's (COCC) 2570-W. This machine was bought, unused, from AMAX Coal, for use at COCC's Muskingum mine. Assembly started in late 1987, and the official start-up came in 1989. The dragline can be operated from either of its twin cabs, depending on which way the machine is working.

Bucyrus-Erie 2570-W
A Bucyrus-Erie 2570-W dragline kicks up a little dust with its 115cu-yd bucket at Drummond Coal's Cedrum Mine in the early 1980s. This is but one of thirty 2570-W units that Bucyrus-Erie had sold worldwide by the end of 1994. In the foreground, a 22cu-yd Marathon LeTourneau L-1200 wheel loader works the lower bench.

Bucyrus-Erie 2570-W
Another view of the Bucyrus-Erie 2570-W, working at the Muskingum mine in December 1993. With its 115cu-yd capacity bucket, suspended from a 335ft twin-boom, it is the principal stripping machine at the mine since Big Muskie was shut down. Note the mechanism that controls the walking action of the dragline. These "shoes" support the entire machines weight of 13,000,000lb (6,500ton), when it travels or "walks", hence the classification of the mach-ine as a walking dragline.

Bucyrus-Erie 4250-W
On May 22, 1969, the Bucyrus-Erie 4250-W walking dragline was officially dedicated into service at Central Ohio Coal Company's Muskingum mine, an operating subsidiary of American Electric Power Co., located near Zanesville, Ohio. The enormous dragline was given the name "Big Muskie." It was a fitting name since the 4250-W was the largest single-bucket digging machine ever created. With a capacity of 220cu-yd, it took the crown of the mightiest earthmover away from the 180cu-yd Marion 6360 stripping shovel. Even though the Marion shovel weighed more, Big Muskie swung the bigger bucket. *Bucyrus-Erie*

Bucyrus-Erie 4250-W
Manufacture of the BE 4250-W commenced in 1966, at Bucyrus-Erie's South Milwaukee plant in Wisconsin. During the next couple of years, approximately 340 rail carloads and 260 truckloads were needed to ship all of Big Muskie's parts to the erection site at the Muskingum mine in Ohio. Even during the field assembly, the big dragline took up an enormous amount of space. From the back of the machine to the tip of the boom in the horizontal position, the 4250-W had a 487ft 6in length, more than one and a half times the length of a football field. *Bucyrus-Erie*

Bucyrus-Erie 4250-W
The BE 4250-W had a maximum digging depth of 185ft. This was just enough, since some of the deepest deposits of coal were uncovered at 182ft. Height to the top of the boom was 222ft 6in, or about 22 stories. Overall working weight when the machine started up was 27,000,000lb (13,500ton), but with added bracing and reinforcements that came later, the truer figure is closer to 14,000tons. The twin-boom on Big Muskie is 310ft long and is filled with the inert gas nitrogen at about 100psi. This is monitored by gauges that indicate the pressure in different sections of the boom. If any cracks or failures develop, the pressure drops. This in turn sets off a series of alarms, alerting crews to potentially serious problems. *Bucyrus-Erie*

Bucyrus-Erie 4250-W

The front of the BE 4250-W shows off the massive cable sheaves, carrying 5in diameter wire rope. The over and under design helps keep the cables from dragging on the ground, where mud and debris could damage the cables' inner pathways and drums. All working movements of the machine were controlled by a single operator, high off the ground in an air-conditioned cab. For a size comparison, note the person exiting the machine at the bottom of the picture. *Frank Page*

Bucyrus-Erie 4250-W

The drag bucket of the 4250-W can easily swallow a Cat D9H and then some. Here the dozer is making an earthen ramp into the bucket so welding trucks can be brought in to make some on-the-spot repairs. If repairs could not be made on location, another of Big Muskie's spare buckets would be brought in to replace the damaged unit. *Frank Page*

Next page
Bucyrus-Erie 4250-W

Looking more like a building than a machine is the housing of BE's 4250-W dragline. Length of the housing itself is 140ft, with a 120ft width (151ft including the walking shoes) and a 67ft height. Each side of the dragline is taken up by the large hydraulic walking system. The total length of a "shoe" is 130ft. It is made in two sections and is pinned in the middle. This allows some flexibility over an uneven surface. Each side has two massive hydraulic lifting cylinders located directly above each section of the walking base. Each step moves the machine backward 14ft. Hydraulic fluid capacity, supplying the entire dragline, including the walking system, is 26,000 gallons. The "tub" that supports Big Muskie when it is working, is 105ft in diameter and 8ft in depth. Power is brought into the 4250-W housing at 13,800volts. This is equivalent, at peak power demand, to about 62,900hp. That's a lot of ponies.

Bucyrus-Erie 4250-W

The business end of the BE 4250-W is its 220cu-yd drag bucket. It is one of three such units used on the machine. Total load capacity rating for the bucket was 320tons. The bucket alone, with its hardware, weighs 460,000lb (230ton). Length was 27ft, width 23ft, with a 14ft basket height and a 23ft arch height. The cables supporting the bucket are 5in diameter wire rope. Each foot of it weighs over 50lb, and there's 3,728ft of cable just for the four main hoist ropes. The combined drag rope lengths total 2,086ft. The buckets were in a state of constant repair, making sure there was at least one ready to replace the machines current unit when it needed rotating (usually every seven to nine months).

Bucyrus-Erie 4250-W

In January 1991, Big Muskie was parked just a few yards away from were it had last been working. With the low demand for high-sulfur coal and other Clean Air Act legislation, the 4250-W's capacity was no longer needed. Shown in December 1993, it sits behind a fence to keep the vandals at bay. With its hydraulic fluid drained, Big Muskie faces north, waiting for the day it will return to work, a day that probably will never come again. In its working lifetime, the 4250-W removed over 608,000,000cu-yd of overburden, uncovering over 20,000,000tons of "clean" coal. And Big Muskie was no stranger to the limelight, having appeared in television episodes of "That's Incredible", "Sesame Street", "PM Magazine", and a BBC documentary in England. Plans are to donate the big dragline to the park service, if all of the red tape can be worked out. It would be unthinkable to let the cutting torches have their way with her. There was only one 4250-W dragline ever built, at a cost of $25million in 1969 dollars. With inflation, the cost of the same machine today would be astronomical!

Bucyrus-Erie 3270-W (Lot-1)

With its 176cu-yd capacity, the 3270-W had a maximum suspended load rating, including the bucket, of 915,000lb on its 330ft twin boom assembly. Height to the top of the boom was 230ft, with an overall machine working weight of 17,435,000lb (8,718ton).

Bucyrus-Erie 3270-W (Lot-2)

The second and last Bucyrus-Erie 3270-W, was the sister machine to the first unit at the Delta Mine. Referred to as the "Lot-2" machine, it started work just a few weeks after the Lot-1 unit in October 1979, at AMAX's Ayrshire Mine, Chandler, Indiana. Both 3270-W draglines share the same basic specifications. They are even painted alike. The quickest way to tell them apart is that the second 3270-W, at Ayrshire, has round ducting vents on its upper rear back and sides. The first machine, at Delta, does not. Shown here working in July 1992 is the second 3270-W.

Upper left
Bucyrus-Erie 3270-W (Lot-2)
Both of the BE 3270-W draglines were marvelous machines, if a bit on the boxy side aesthetically. Both also share the title of second-largest draglines in the world. In December 1993, the surface operations were shut down at the Ayrshire Mine, and the Lot-2 BE 3270-W was parked. Plans to dismantle and move the big machine out west, to the Powder River Basin, are under consideration by the draglines' owners, Cyprus Amax Minerals Co. At the time of this writing, no decision had been reached.

Lower left
Bucyrus-Erie 2570-WS
The largest dragline currently operating in the Powder River Basin region of Wyoming is the Bucyrus-Erie 2570-WS "Ursa Major" of Thunder Basin Coal Company, at the company's Black Thunder Mine. The mighty Ursa Major has a 160cu-yd bucket on a 360ft boom, making it the fourth-largest capacity dragline ever produced, right behind the BE 4250-W and the two BE 3270-W machines. Assembly started on the 2570-WS in March 1991, and it was ready for work in February 1993.

Bucyrus-Erie 3270-W (Lot-2)
This is the 176cu-yd capacity spare bucket belonging to the BE 3270-W Lot-2 dragline, at the AMAX Ayrshire Mine in Indiana. Only one bucket was kept in reserve, as compared to the two 220cu-yd back-up units for the BE 4250-W "Big Muskie" dragline.

Bucyrus-Erie 2570-WS

The 160cu-yd capacity, 19ft wide bucket of the Bucyrus-Erie 2570-WS "Ursa Major" is very unique. It is the largest of Bucyrus-Erie's special patented High Production System (HPS) designed buckets. Through the extensive use of computer-aided finite element design, substantial weight savings were achieved, without sacrificing the structural integrity of the bucket. This translates to a larger capacity and a 675,000lb suspended load rating, including the bucket and its hardware weight. During lunch and any other shift change shutdown, mine personnel inspect the bucket's hardware and pins for any possible damage and wear problems. Note how the material the dragline has been handling has polished the inner bucket surfaces to almost a mirror-like finish.

Bucyrus-Erie 2570-WS

As you can see, the BE 2570-WS (S stands for "super") is a very large machine, weighing in at 14,710,000lb (7,355ton), though the housing looks more like a warehouse, than a dragline. The structure on top houses the large air filtering system, necessary to keep internal temperature and dust problems as low as possible.

P&H/Page 757

Around 1987, the Harnischfeger Corporation (P&H) purchased the Page Engineering Co., one of the pioneers in the development of walking draglines. At the time of the purchase, the largest dragline Page had produced was its model 757, with rated capacities in the 50-80cu-yd range. Though a larger capacity 9100 series had been designed, none had ever been built. Pictured, is a 757 series machine delivered in 1983 to Obed Mountain Coal Co. Ltd., located in the foothills of the Canadian Rockies, near Hinton, Alberta. This model was equipped with a 75cu-yd bucket, on a 291ft boom. Total operating weight of the dragline was 9,000,000lb (4,500ton). *Harnischfeger Corp.*

Right
P&H 2355 DE

Only a few manufacturers make today's large crawler draglines. One such machine is Harnischfeger Corporation's P&H 2355 DE. First introduced in 1981, the model line has been a slow but steady seller. The dragline is available as an all-electric-powered machine or a diesel-electric, such as the version pictured, operating at Bloomfield Collieries, New Castle, New South Wales, Australia. This machine went into service around 1986, equipped with a 20cu-yd bucket, on a 160ft boom, with a maximum suspended load rating of 100,000lb. Power for the electric AC/DC generators is supplied by two Cat D3512, V-12 diesel engines, with an output rating of 2400 gross hp @ 1800rpm. Operating weight of this version is 1,484,000lb (742ton), and it is carried on two crawlers with 36ft lengths. *Harnischfeger Corp.*

P&H 757

The first of the 757 series draglines built entirely by Harnischfeger was the P&H 757 "Ace of Spades", for British Coal Opencast's Stobswood Mine, Northumberland, in the United Kingdom. Officially commissioned in December 1991, the Ace of Spades went into full operation in February 1992. This model is equipped with a 65cu-yd bucket on a 310ft boom. Though this 757 is capable of taking a larger 75cu-yd bucket, the owners wanted to underrate it to ensure a trouble-free stay during the mine's anticipated twelve-year life span. Total operating weight of the machine is 8,834,000lb (4,417ton). The Ace of Spades is now the largest operating dragline in Europe, since the 65cu-yd Bucyrus-Erie 1550-W Big Geordie was shut down. *Harnischfeger Corp.*

Marion 305-M

The largest two-crawler dragline in the world is the Marion 305-M. The order for the first unit was received in 1989, and it was ready for work at Northern Waggons' coal mine, in New South Wales, Australia, in June 1991. The first 305-M was a diesel-electric version, powered by a single 2145fhp diesel engine driving the electrical generators. This machine is equipped with a 22cu-yd bucket on a 225ft boom, with a suspended load rating of 100,000lb. Maximum capacity designed for the 305-M dragline is 24cu-yd, on a 195ft boom, with a 120,000lb load rating. Weight of the big Marion is 2,500,000lb (1,250ton). This is carried by two enormous crawlers, each of which is 44ft long and almost 12ft wide. *Marion INDRESCO*

Left

Manitowoc 6400

Better known for its extensive heavy lift crane line, Manitowoc Engineering Company of Wisconsin also produces a line of draglines. Based on modular components from its crane product line, the draglines have established a very loyal following by mine and quarry owners the world over. Largest of these machines is the Manitowoc 6400 series, introduced in 1977. With a 15cu-yd bucket, on a 160ft boom, the 6400 has a maximum suspended load capacity of 80,000lb. The main power source is a single Cummins KTA-3067-C1600 V-16, rated at 1600fhp @ 2000rpm. A separate 450fhp Cummins six-cylinder engine powers the lower works. The average operating weight of the 6400 is 1,107,720lb (554ton). *Manitowoc Engineering*

Marion 195-M

Introduced in the early 1970s, the Marion 195-M crawler dragline is based on the company's very successful 191-M series of mining shovels. The dragline is rated for 13-17cu-yd bucket capacities, with boom lengths of 130-210ft. Overall working weight is 1,450,000lb (725ton). A yellow Marion 195-M is pictured working in January 1978, at Carter Mining Company's Rawhide Mine, near Gillette, Wyoming. Today, the Rawhide Mine is operated by the Powder River Coal Company. *Marion INDRESCO*

CHAPTER 4

The Hydraulic Excavators

UNTIL THE MID-1950s, THE WORLD excavator market had been dominated by cable-operated types of machines. But in 1954, the German company of Demag (Deutsche Maschinenfabrik AG) released the first "fully" hydraulic, crawler-mounted production excavator in the world, the B-504. This was a relatively small machine, since suitable hydraulic components were not available, and it used a still young and emerging technology. But it wouldn't be long before the hydraulic machines would replace the small- to mid-size shovel and backhoe cable models that the industry had depended on for some time.

In 1971, the French firm of Poclain introduced the first fully hydraulic mining excavator to the world market, the 151ton EC1000. In 1975, this machine was released in an updated version as the 179ton 1000CK Series I. It was not long, however, before the German manufacturers regained world leadership in this class of machines.

SMEC 4500
The largest hydraulic excavator ever produced in Japan was the gigantic SMEC 4500 front shovel. This was the second machine line introduced by SMEC—the Surface Mining Equipment for Coal Technology Research Association—after the massive SMEC Wheel Loader in 1986. The SMEC 4500 was developed jointly by Mitsubishi Heavy Industries and Kobe Steel, Ltd., and was built at Kobe's Takasago Works. The big mining shovel was powered by two 1210hp diesel engines, with a combined rating of 2420 gross hp @ 1800rpm. The bucket capacity range was from 19.6 to 39.2cu-yd, with a maximum digging, eight of 61ft 4in. The overall working weight was 926,000lb (463ton), and it was carried on 31ft 4in-long crawlers. Height to the top of the operator's cab was 29ft. The only unit ever manufactured was delivered for field trial testing by BHP-Utah at the Blackwater Mine in Queensland's Bowen basin, Australia, in November 1987. It was matched up to a new fleet of 200ton capacity LeTourneau T-2200 Titan haulers. Even though the shovel performed extremely well, after the breakup of the eleven companies making up the SMEC group, the SMEC 4500 front shovel was dismantled and scrapped at the end of 1992 for liability reasons. *Kobe Steel, Ltd.*

O&K RH300

One of the world leaders in the design and manufacturing of large hydraulic excavators is Orenstein & Koppel of Germany, better known as O&K. In 1979, O&K released their famous RH300 hydraulic front shovel, which, at the time, was the largest ever manufactured. The first RH300, a low-cab version, went to work for Northern Strip Mining Ltd. (NSM) at its Donnington Extension in the United Kingdom, matched to WABCO 170C Haulpak rear dumps. Around 1981, the big excavator was moved to NSM's Godkine Coal Mine in Derbyshire. This first machine was powered by two Cummins KTA2300-C1200 diesel engines, with combined total power ratings of 2400 gross hp/2320fhp @ 1950rpm. The NSM machine weighed in at 1,098,000lb (549ton) when equipped with its standard 29cu-yd capacity bucket. *Orenstein & Koppel*

O&K RH120C
One of the most popular O&K excavators, in the very competitive 200ton-plus weight machine category, is the RH120C model, introduced in 1983. The RH120C is equipped with a standard 17cu-yd capacity bucket on a boom that incorporates O&K's exclusive TriPower system for maintaining a constant bucket angle during all digging applications. The shovel is powered by two Cummins KTTA19-C700 diesel engines, rated at 1400 gross hp @ 2100rpm and 1180fhp @ 1800rpm. The standard front shovel version of this model weighs in at 485,010lb (243ton).

Left
O&K RH300E
The second O&K RH300E, an electric version, was delivered to Codelco's Chuquicamata Copper Mine in Chile in 1987. Similar in design to the first unit, this version had a high-mounted cab. Power was supplied by two 900kW electric motors, producing a total of 2414hp. This machine also came equipped with a larger 34cu-yd capacity rock bucket. The operating weight had also increased to 1,132,000lb (566ton). This RH300E now sits idle, parked due to a slowdown in production at the mine. Only three RH300 front shovels were ever built, with only two of the units ever being delivered. The third was never sold and was used for spare parts on the first two machines. *Orenstein & Koppel*

The German firms were quick to see the potential of large hydraulic mining excavators in the marketplace. Orenstein & Koppel (O&K), which produced their first hydraulic excavator in 1961, released their popular 150ton RH75 in 1975, then followed it with the mammoth RH300 in 1979. Liebherr, which produced its first hydraulic machine in 1957, introduced its 182ton R991 in 1977. This was followed by the R992 and R994 machines of the 1980s. Mannesmann Demag released their H241 in 1978, later upgraded to the H285 in 1986. That same year, Demag introduced the H485—which is still the largest hydraulic excavator series in the world.

American manufacturers also had the ability to produce large excavators, though not necessarily as massive as the German machines. The 130ton Koehring 1266D, released in 1973, was the first large hydraulic machine produced by a US firm. It was later replaced by the 154ton 1466FS model. Harnischfeger introduced its 200ton P&H 1200 in 1978, and it was later updated to a 1200B variation before being replaced by the 1550 series in 1989. In 1981, the Bucyrus-Erie Company threw

O&K RH120C

What's the fastest way to get from one side of the mine site to the other? Why, in the back of the 350ton capacity Terex 33-19 Titan, of course! This O&K RH120C saved six hours of down time by hitching a ride to its new work site, located within Westar's Balmer mining operation. The current backhoe version of the RH120C is equipped with a 17cu-yd capacity bucket and has the same power output as the front shovel model, 1180fhp. The weight of the backhoe is a little less than that of the shovel at 483,690lb (242ton). *Bruce Kurschenska*

O&K RH170

The newest member of O&K's large mining excavator line is their RH170, introduced at the April 1995 Bauma mining show in Germany. Powered by two Cummins KT38-C925 diesel engines, output is rated at 1850 gross hp @ 2100rpm and 1662fhp @ 1800rpm. Standard bucket capacity is 27.5cu-yds for the shovel and 26cu-yds for the backhoe version. Maximum digging height is 48ft 5in. Standard operating weight is 749,560lb (375ton). *Orenstein & Koppel*

O&K RH200
Today, the largest hydraulic front shovel produced by O&K is their RH200 excavator. The first 26cu-yd machine was delivered in 1989 to Budge Mining, West Chevington, Northumberland, in the United Kingdom. The RH200 is powered by two Cummins KTA38-C1200 diesel engines, rated at 2400 gross hp @ 2100rpm and 2102fhp @ 1800rpm. Standard bucket capacity is 34cu-yd, but the version shown here, which started working in a Pennsylvania coal mine in 1991, is equipped with a 29cu-yd bullclam. Height to the top of the cab is 26ft, and each crawler section is just over 28ft in length.

their hat into the ring with the 112ton 500-H, followed by the 140ton 550-HS of 1982. Of all of the early American efforts, the Marion 3560 series machines of 1981 were by far the largest, weighing in at 307tons.

The large Japanese equipment manufacturers were late in introducing large mining excavators to the industry, but when they did, they brought with them a wealth of technological know-how and marketing savvy. The Hitachi UH801, weighing as much as 175ton, led the way in 1979. Next came Komatsu with the 176ton PC1500-1, introduced in 1981. (It was replaced by the PC1600 in the late 1980s.) Mitsubishi showcased its prototype 182ton MS1600 in the early 1980s, and Kobelco, working with the SMEC group of Japanese companies, produced the largest hydraulic excavator ever to come out of Japan, the gigantic 463ton SMEC 4500, in 1987.

The large hydraulic excavator has proven its productivity value in mining operations the world over. But which is superior, the large electric cable shovels or their hydraulic counterparts? It really depends on the mine layout, material being handled, and projected life span of the operation. You wouldn't want to invest in an expensive cable machine if your gold mine would be depleted in seven years. On the other hand, if your coal operations are expected to last fifteen years, then a hydraulic shovel, with half the life expectancy of its cable counterpart, is definitely not the best choice. A large cable shovel quite often lasts 100,000 hours or more while a hydraulic machine's useful life is in the range of 40,000–60,000 hours. The hydraulic shovel cost less, but the cable version has greater digging capacity.

Often the best answer is a combination of both machines, working at different stages in the mining operation. Whatever the choice, it looks like the large hydraulic mining excavators are here to stay.

O&K RH200
Though not as large as their previous RH300 model, the O&K RH200, weighing in at 1,040,570lb (520ton), is still one of the largest hydraulic shovels available to the world mining market. The RH200 is best suited to loading haulers in the 150-200ton range, though the unit is capable of handling even larger trucks. Here, the shovel is loading a 150ton capacity Caterpillar 785 rear dump hauler. Maximum standard digging height is 50ft in hard rock applications.

O&K RH200E

O&K's current big hydraulic excavator is also available in an all-electric-powered form, known as the RH200E. Power is provided by one electric motor, with a combined total rated output of 1600kW/2146hp. Shown here is one of two backhoe versions (both electric) of the RH200E delivered in October 1991 to Amcoal's Kleinkopje Colliery mine in South Africa. Maximum bucket capacity for the backhoe version is 30cu-yd. *Orenstein & Koppel*

Left

Demag H241

Mannesmann Demag Baumaschinen of Germany released its very popular Demag H241 excavator in 1978. It was a trend setter in many ways, especially in size. The H241 was powered by a single GM 16V-149T sixteen-cylinder diesel engine, rated at 1350 gross hp/1290fhp. Standard front shovel bucket capacity was rated at 19cu-yd, with an optional 28cu-yd coal version available. A backhoe model was also offered. Maximum digging height was almost 51ft. Total operating weight of the shovel was 620,000lb (310ton). Shown here in 1986 at Syncrude Canada Ltd. oil sands operation in Alberta, is a H241 loading a Marathon LeTourneau (now LeTourneau, Inc.) 33-15C Titan hauler. These were some of the first trucks produced by LeTourneau after they bought the Titan hauler line from General Motors in 1985.

Demag H285

In 1986, the Demag H285 was introduced as a replacement for the H241 model. Available in either a front shovel or a backhoe variation, the big excavator is powered by a Cummins KTTA50C sixteen-cylinder diesel engine, rated at 1675fhp at 1800rpm. Standard bucket capacity for the current H285S front shovel is 25cu-yd, with the backhoe version having a 23cu-yd unit. Maximum weight of the machine is 738,500lb (369ton). Pictured is a H285 backhoe, working at the Hebden Mine in Australia. *Mannesmann Demag Baumaschinen*

Demag H485

In 1986, Demag introduced its gigantic H485 hydraulic front shovel. This machine is the largest of its type in the world. The first unit (shown here) was powered by a single Daimler-Benz MTU 16V-396TC43 diesel engine, rated at 2103fhp @ 1800rpm. This H485 was equipped with a 30cu-yd capacity bullclam when it was delivered to Coal Contractors Ltd. at their Roughcastle site in Scotland. Height to the top of the cab is 30ft, and the upperworks rides on crawlers that are 34ft in length, with 9ft 3in heights. Total operating weight of the early H485 was 1,200,000lb (600ton). *Mannesmann Demag Baumaschinen*

Demag H485SE

Today, the Demag is available in an upgraded H485S version. Standard power is now supplied by two Cummins KTTA50C sixteen-cylinder diesel engines, with a maximum rated output of 3590 gross hp @ 2100rpm, and 3000fhp @ 1800rpm. Pictured is an electric-powered version, the H485SE, rated at 2100kW/2850hp from its 4160volt Siemens 60-cycle electric motor. This example was the sixteenth machine sold by the company and the first Demag H485S sold in the United States. It started operations in August 1993, at Magma Copper Company's Pinto Valley Mine in Miami, Arizona. Equipped with a 44cu-yd bullclam, it could load one of the mine's 190ton capacity Haulpak 685E haulers in three quick passes. This version of the shovel weighs in at 1,410,000lb (705ton). *Mannesmann Demag Corp.*

Left
Demag H485SE

The only US version of the Demag H485SE, is shown hard at work under the hot Arizona sun. With a maximum digging height of 61ft 4in for its 44cu-yd bucket, the H485 series competes directly with cable shovels having similar capacities. Working in restricted areas, such as up against the face of the pit wall, is work well suited to the design of this large hydraulic shovel. *Mannesmann Demag Corp.*

Upper left
Demag H485
The Demag H485 is also available in a backhoe configuration, making it the largest available in the world. The first unit was a diesel-powered version, delivered in February 1990, to Saxonville Coal, in Australia. It was equipped with a 34cu-yd bucket. This can load the mine's 190ton haulers in four passes. *Mannesmann Demag Baumaschinen*

Lower left
Demag H455S
At the April 1995 Bauma show in Germany, Demag announced its latest big mining excavator, the 33cu-yd capacity H455S. Weighing in at 1,000,000lb (500ton), the new Demag has its sights set clearly on the O&K RH200 market. The H455S is powered by two Cummins KTTA-38C twelve-cylinder diesel engines, for a combined rated output of 2692 gross hp @ 2100rpm and 2250fhp @ 1800rpm. Height to the top of the cab is 28ft 7in, with a 30ft crawler length. *Mannesmann Demag Corp.*

Demag H485SE
At the end of November 1994, the first US Demag H485SE was moved from the Pinto Valley Mine to ASARCO's Ray complex in Hayden, Arizona. The big shovel was put back to work in December, this time loading 240ton capacity Haulpak 830E haulers. *Mannesmann Demag Corp.*

Liebherr R996

A few years ago, Liebherr started development of an ultra-large excavator, but found the world economic recession of the early 1990s a good reason to delay the creation of such a beast. With an improving economic climate, however, the time is now right for the release of Liebherr's biggest machine, the R996 Litronic. Officially announced in April 1995, the first unit was unveiled in May 1995 at its excavator factory in France. Power is supplied by two Cummins K1800E sixteen-cylinder diesel engines, with a combined output of 3000fhp @ 1800rpm. Equipped with a 36.6cu-yd bullclam and weighing in at 1,168,400lb (584ton), the Liebherr is second only in terms of size to Demag's H485 series of excavators. The first R996 sold in the United States was a barge-mounted backhoe version for dredging operations. *Liebherr-France*

Left
Liebherr R994

Most examples of hydraulic shovels are available in backhoe configurations, such as this Liebherr R994, working at a limestone quarry in the Netherlands. Basic specifications are the same as its shovel counterpart. Bucket capacity is up to 23.5cu-yd for the backhoe version, with a working weight of 471,800lb (236ton). *Liebherr-France*

Right
Demag H485SP (H685SP)

The latest version of Demag's mammoth excavator is the H485SP. It is the largest and most powerful hydraulic shovel presently in use today. The first of these new giants was delivered to Klemke & Son Construction Ltd., in Alberta, Canada and commissioned in March 1995, boasting a 46cu-yd, 70ton capacity bullclam. Power is supplied by two Caterpillar 3516DI-TA diesel engines, for a combined rated output of 4000ftp @ 1800rpm. Total operating weight for this version is 1,500,000lb (750ton). This series of machines was originally going to be identified as the H685SP, but it was decided by Demag to stay within the H485 model family nomenclature after the first machine was delivered. *Mannesmann Demag Corp.*

Liebherr R994

Another large producer of hydraulic mining shovels from Germany is the Liebherr group of companies. Introduced around 1985, the current Liebherr R994 is powered by a single Cummins KTTA38-C1350 twelve-cylinder diesel engine, with a maximum rating of 1256gross hp @ 2100rpm and 1126fhp @ 1800rpm. The front shovel has a bucket capacity load range of 13.7-23.5cu-yd and a working weight of 487,900lb (244-ton), placing it in one of the industry's most competitive class of mining machines. The unit pictured is working at a marl quarry in Belgium. *Liebherr-France*

Marion 3560

In 1981, Marion, then a division of Dresser Industries, launched its 3560 series of hydraulic mining shovels. At the time, these were the largest machines ever produced by a US manufacturer. Shown here in February 1986 is Muskingum Mining Company's Marion 3560 shovel, loading a 95ton capacity Caterpillar 777B. *Marion INDRESCO*

Marion 3560

Available engine power options for the Marion 3560 were two Cat 3412PCTA diesels, rated at 1400fhp, or two Cummins VTA28-C725, V-12 diesels, rated at 1410fhp @ 1800rpm. Electric-powered versions were also available. Standard bucket capacity was 22cu-yd, with a load range of 15-32cu-yd for the 3560B version. Maximum digging height of the front shovel was 46ft 9in, with a total operating weight of 614,000lb (307ton). Height to the top of the operator's cab is almost 22ft. Vigo Coal's 3560 shovel is shown here removing overburden from on top of a coal seam in April 1988. *Marion INDRESCO*

Marion 3560

Along with the front shovel versions of the 3560, Marion produced a few of the excavators equipped as backhoe models. Standard engines were two Cat 3412PCTA diesels, with a combined rating of 1400fhp @ 1800rpm; electric-powered machines were also available. Standard bucket capacity was rated at 18cu-yd, with an optional 27cu-yd coal-loading version. Maximum reach of the backhoe was 60ft. Total operating weight was 656,000lb (328ton), carried on crawlers with 26ft 5in lengths. The first two backhoe units were delivered to Teck Industries' Bullmoose Coal Mine, in British Columbia, Canada. One was diesel-powered (pictured), and the other was an all-electric version, both equipped with 16cu-yd buckets. In 1989, the Marion hydraulic line was discontinued after the last two hydraulic 3560B excavators, produced for AOKI Marine Company of Japan, were delivered. Both of these units were yellow, barge-mounted backhoe versions, equipped with 23.5cu-yd buckets. In total, only eight Marion 3560s were produced. *Marion INDRESCO*

P&H 1200B

The Harnischfeger Corporation, better known for its electric mining shovels, also produces a range of hydraulic excavators. First introduced in 1978, the first P&H 1200 series of hydraulic mining machines was produced in Dortmund, Germany. Manufacturing was later shifted to the United States. Power was supplied by two Cummins diesel engines, with a combined rated output of 860fhp @ 1800rpm. Standard capacity for the shovel version was 13cu-yd, with a total operating weight of 415,000lb (208ton). Shown here in a photo from around 1987 is a P&H 1200B operated by Cheveron Resource Company at one of its phosphate mines near Vernal, Utah. *Harnischfeger Corp.*

Right
P&H 2250

The largest hydraulic excavator produced by Harnischfeger is their P&H 2250, introduced in September 1990. The 2250 is an immense machine, weighing in at 745,000lb (373ton). It is powered by a single Cat 3516, V-16 diesel, rated at 2000 gross hp/1800fhp @ 1800rpm. The shovel's bucket capacity is in the 15-33cu-yd range, with a maximum digging height of 57ft. Pictured in 1991 is the first P&H 2250, equipped with a 23cu-yd bullclam, loading a 150ton capacity Caterpillar 785 hauler, at Gold Fields Mining Corporation's Chimney Creek mine in northern Nevada. An upgraded 2250 Series "A" version was introduced in October 1994 with many engine and control improvements adding to the machine's overall productivity. *Harnischfeger Corp.*

P&H 1550

The P&H 1550 is the second-largest excavator currently offered by Harnischfeger, replacing its older 1200B model line. The 1550 is powered by a single Cummins KTTA38C-1350 twelve-cylinder diesel engine, rated at 1350 gross hp/1100fhp. Bucket capacity ranges from 12 to 20cu-yd. Total operating weight of the shovel is 458,000lb (229ton). The first unit was delivered in 1989 to Cyprus Minerals Company's molybdenum mine north of Las Vegas, Nevada, equipped with a 15cu-yd bullclam. *Harnischfeger Corp.*

P&H 2250
In 1993, Harnischfeger delivered its first backhoe version of its P&H 2250, equipped with a 22cu-yd bucket, to the Quintette Mine in British Columbia, Canada. This machine is also an electric-powered model, driven by a single 1200kW/1609hp electric motor. Bucket capacity for the backhoe version is in the 18-32cu-yd range, with a maximum 63ft 4in boom reach. Total operating weight of the backhoe version is 770,000lb (385ton). *Harnischfeger Corp.*

Right
Caterpillar 5130 ME
The first backhoe version (ME) of the Caterpillar 5130 was introduced in late 1993. Sharing the same basic specifications as its shovel counterpart, the ME version has a working range of 10.2-17.8cu-yd capacity buckets, with the largest intended for coal loading applications. Weight of the ME version is 390,000lb (195ton). ME stands for "Mass Excavator." *Oxford Mining Co.*

Caterpillar 5130

At the October 1992 American Mining Congress show in Las Vegas, Nevada, Caterpillar unveiled its new 5130 series hydraulic mining excavator. This was the first front shovel that Cat had designed from the ground up for hard rock applications. Previous designs were based on existing excavator platforms in their line-up, such as the 235 and 245 models. The Cat 5130 is powered by Caterpillar's own 3508, V-8 diesel engine, with a power output of 815 gross hp/755fhp. Standard bucket capacity for the shovel version is rated at 13.75cu-yd. Total operating weight of the 5130 is 385,000lb (193ton). *Caterpillar Inc.*

Caterpillar 5230

With the first unit undergoing early preliminary prototype testing in Idaho, the Caterpillar 5230 hydraulic excavator was officially announced in August 1994. This is the third model introduced in Cat's new series of hydraulic machines, after the 5130 and the 5080 excavators. But this is no lightweight contender. The 5230 is very similar in size and capacity to the now-discontinued Dresser/Marion 3560. The 5230 is powered by a single Cat 3516, V-16 diesel engine, rated at 1575 gross hp and 1470fhp @ 1750rpm. The standard rated bucket capacity for the front shovel is 18.3-22.2cu-yd, with a maximum digging height of almost 49ft. A backhoe version (ME) is also offered, with a maximum capacity bucket size of 31cu-yd. Total operating weight of the 5230 is 693,800lb (347ton). *Caterpillar Inc.*

Right
Hitachi EX3500

The largest hydraulic excavator produced by Hitachi is its EX3500 series, introduced in 1987. The EX3500 is one of the most sophisticated machines on the market and is a big seller worldwide, including the United States. The Super-EX3500-2 version of this excavator was introduced in 1991. The Super-EX is powered by two Cummins KT38-C925 diesel engines, rated at 1760 gross hp/1634fhp @ 1800rpm. Bucket capacity range is from 23.5 to 32.7cu-yd, with a 56ft digging height. Standard operating weight is 728,000lb (364ton). Height to the top of the cab is 22ft 6in, with crawler lengths of 28ft 6in. Like all of the big Hitachi shovels, a backhoe version is also available for the EX3500. Pictured is the large Hitachi loading a 209.5ton-capacity Euclid R-190 hauler. *Euclid-Hitachi*

Hitachi EX1800

In 1987, Hitachi Construction Machinery Co., Ltd., of Japan officially released its new "Giant-EX" series of mining excavators. The Hitachi EX1800 is the second-largest in the series, replacing the company's successful UH801 model line. The EX1800 is powered by two Cummins KTA19-C525 six-cylinder diesel engines, producing 920 gross hp @ 1800rpm. The "Super-EX" released in 1991 is rated at 1000 gross hp. Bucket capacities range from 13.5 to 19cu-yd, with a maximum digging height of 47ft 9in. Total operating weight is 390,000lb (195ton).

CHAPTER 5

The Bucket Wheel Excavators

THE LARGEST TYPES OF EXCAVATORS in the world are the monstrous bucket wheel excavators (BWE) produced in Germany. These machines, with their circular, multiple-bucket digging wheels, are some of the largest mobile land machines in existence. The largest of these, with a daily output of 314,000cu-yd (240,000cu-m), are the units produced by O&K, MAN and Krupp Fördertechnik and working at Rheinbraun's Hambach lignite mine in Germany. The last two excavators delivered with this capacity rating were the Krupp/Buckau-Wolf 14,546ton BWE 291, in 1983, and O&K's 14,877ton BWE 292, in 1991. Both have 71ft-diameter bucket wheels. In total, there are six large BWEs at this mine, and an order was placed in December 1991 for a seventh unit, a 240,000cu-m range MAN/Takraf BWE 293, slated for a late-1995 start-up date.

Rheinbraun operates more than twenty-four large BWEs of varied capacities at five different mine sites. Other machines in the ultra-large-capacity category include: a 14,326ton Buckau-Wolf 200,000cu-m BWE 287 that started operating in 1976; a 14,028ton O&K 240,000cu-m BWE 289 that started operating in 1978; a 14,546ton Krupp 240,000cu-m BWE 288, first used in 1978, and a 14,500ton MAN 240,000cu-m BWE 290.

In the last few years, the four major producers of BWE-type machines in Germany have consolidated into just two companies. Buckau-Wolf, a producer of this type of excavator for

O&K BWE 292
Here is the front row of eight crawlers of the excavator section of the O&K 292. Like the Krupp machines before it, the entire unit has fifteen crawler units, all the same size as the Krupp versions. The O&K 292 would be the last ultra-large bucket wheel excavator the company would ever build. By mid-1992, the Plants and Systems division of O&K, which built the BWEs, was sold to their main competitor, Krupp Industrietechnik GmbH, of Germany, since renamed Krupp Fördertechnik. *Orenstein & Koppel*

Bucyrus-Erie/Marion 5872-WX

The 5872-WX is a hybrid of sorts, combining a new Bucyrus-Erie bucket wheel excavator (BWE), with the lower works of a parked stripping shovel, a Marion 5860 from CONSOL's Truax Traer Burning Star No. 3 mine. Production started on the BWE in early 1985 at the Captain Mine in southwest Illinois, and it was ready for operation by the end of February 1986.

more than forty-five years, became a part of Krupp Industrietechnik GmbH in 1983, when the Buckau-Walther group, the holding company of Buckau-Wolf, was integrated into Krupp. O&K's Plants and Systems division, builder of BWEs since 1934, was sold in mid-1992 to Hoesch AG, which merged with Fried Krupp AG, the majority shareholder and parent company of Krupp Industrietechnik (since renamed Krupp Fördertechnik).

The last major manufacturer of large BWEs, Lauchhammer, can trace its origins back to 1725, and until recently it was part of the Mannesmann Demag group of companies. In the

Left

Bucyrus-Erie/Marion 5872-WX

The main purpose of the 5872-EX is to remove the uppermost layers of top soil and clay off the coal seam and then deposit the overburden in the spoil piles across the pit. Its cross-pit conveyor can deposit the material much further away from the actual working area than can a shovel. This enables the shovels to work in deeper conditions and to lessen the chance of spoil pile slides into the pit. The 5872-WX measures 716ft across, from the digging wheel to the end of the conveyer. The excavator reaches 250ft into the air at its highest point and weighs in at 10,763,000lb (5382ton). Since the destruction of the 180cu-yd Marion 6360, the 5872-WX is now working in conjunction with the mine's Marion 5900 stripping shovel.

O&K BWE 289
The largest man-made earthmoving machines operating today are the incredible "Central Tower" type bucket wheel excavators (BWE) of Germany. The largest of these is the 314,000cu-yd (240,000cu-m) daily output class of machines operating for Rheinische Braun-kohlenwerke AG, better known as Rheinbraun, at its Hambach lignite mine. Shown here is the 14,028ton O&K BWE 289, which was assembled on-site between 1974 and 1977. *Krupp Fördertechnik*

late 1980s, however, Demag sold the division to Takraf, forming the new company of Takraf-Lauchhammer GmbH. The largest machines produced by this company are their SRs 6300 series of BWEs, of which three have been built, all of them at work in Germany. This series of machines weighs in at about 9,753ton each, considerably smaller than the giants produced by Krupp and O&K but still large enough to dwarf most other mining equipment. Takraf is currently in a joint effort with the German firm of MAN in the production of a 240,000cu-m BWE for Reinbraun. It is due for completion in 1995.

In the United States, the Bucyrus-Erie Company really is the only producer of large BWEs. The company built their first unit in the late 1940s by mounting the excavator unit onto a conventional stripping shovel's lower works. In 1954, Bucyrus-Erie introduced the 934-WX, its first BWE designed and built from the ground up. This led to the production of a small number of machines with varied capacity outputs, and most of them were put to work in the Illinois Basin coal-producing regions. The largest of these was the BE 5872-WX, produced for Arch Minerals' Captain Mine in 1986. However, the top portion was a new BE excavator while the lower part was the modified lower-works of a used Marion 5860 stripping shovel

Next page
Krupp BWE 288
Weighing in at 29,092,000lb (14,546ton), the giant Krupp BWE 288 outweighs even the largest stripping shovels and draglines. Average length of the excavator and its loader is over 700ft, carried on fifteen mammoth crawlers. BWE 288 was the first 240,000cu-m daily output machine Krupp built in this size class. *Krupp Fördertechnik*

Krupp/O&K BWE 285
Here is the business end of the 13,367ton Krupp/O&K BWE 285, a 200,000cu-m daily output machine at the Rheinbraun Fortuna mine. This machine was as ordered in 1972 and started full operations in 1976. Looking more like a giant circular saw, the bucket wheel is 71 ft in diameter and is driven by electric motors. It takes over 3360kW/4506hp just to drive the wheel alone! Today, this BWE operates at Rheinbraun's Tagebau Garzweiler mine. *Krupp Fördertechnik*

formerly owned by CONSOL Coal.

Utilization of a few of the German-style BWEs has been tried in the United States but with mixed results. Larger glacial boulders encountered in many North American mining sites severely hampered the effectiveness of these types of machines. In 1961, Peabody Coal Co. tried out a medium-capacity Krupp BWE at one of its Illinois mines. In 1978, Arch Mineral tried using some O&K machines at its Captain Mine. In the end, however, all of these machines proved ineffective. The German designs were intended to dig softer, sandier material, not the hard, rocky material found in most mining areas in this country.

But in 1993, Carter Mining Company's Caballo mine put a Krupp BWE into use, the first such machine used in the Powder River Basin mining area of Wyoming for overburden removal. To help with the management of large rocks and clay deposits, classifiers—nose-like projections—were attached to each bucket of the 36ft diameter wheel. This limits the size of rocks the bucket can carry to about 2ft. Anything larger will cause the machine real trouble. If this machine works out, however, maybe we'll see more of these incredible excavators at work in this country in the years to come.

O&K BWE 292

The largest BWE ever built was produced by Orenstein & Koppel (O&K) and was the fifth such machine delivered in the 240,000cu-m class of BWEs produced by German manufacturers. Assembly on the O&K 292 started at Rheinbraun's Hambach mine in September 1988 and was completed in February 1991. Highest point is 295ft off the ground and the entire excavator weighs in at 29,754,000lb (14,877ton), more than any other BWE that came before the 292. It takes a total of five people to operate the entire system. It is also the first machine in its class to have advanced computer software programs that help the operators achieve the best digging results, with controls that have the ability to "learn." This enables the machine to make quick changes in its digging pattern, based on the deposit conditions. Early production reports indicate that this BWE is the most productive at the Hambach mine. O&K 292 would join another family member, the O&K 289, that has been in operation since 1978. It too, is a 240,000cu-m daily output BWE. *Orenstein & Koppel*

Krupp BWE 288

The front crawler set on the Krupp BWE 288 consists of eight units for the front row and four for the rear set on the excavator section. The loader carries three sets, for a total of fifteen crawlers for the entire machine. Each crawler is 49ft long, 10ft high, and 12ft wide. These giant tracks are necessary to reduce the overall ground pressure a machine of this size can exert. Anything less and the unit would just sink into the ground and get itself stuck. *Krupp Fördertechnik*

Index